G000079250

Born To Sta[nd Out]

Not to Fit In

Empower Yourself To Live
An Extraordinary Life

Teuta Avdyli

Born To Stand Out, Not To Fit In.
Empower Yourself To Live An Extraordinary Life

Author Name: Teuta Avdyli

Copyright © 2019 Teuta Avdyli

All rights reserved. No part of this document may be reproduced or transmitted in any form whatsoever, electronic, or mechanical, including photocopying, recording, or by any informational storage or retrieval system of any nature without the express written, dated and signed permission of the author.

ISBN: 9781098986445

Book Design & Book Writing Coaching & Publishing done by:

Brand for Speakers
www.brandforspeakers.com
Limits of liability / disclaimer of warranty: The author and publisher of this book have used their best efforts in preparing this material. The author and publisher make no representation or warranties with respect to the accuracy, applicability, or completeness of the contents. They disclaim any warranties (express or implied), merchantability for any particular purpose. The author and publisher shall in no event be held liable for any loss or other damages, including but not limited to special, incidental, consequential, or other damages. The information presented in this publication is compiled from sources believed to be accurate, however, the publishers assume no responsibility for errors or omissions. The information in this publication is not intended to replace or substitute professional advice. The author and publisher specifically disclaim any liability, loss, or risk that is incurred as a consequence, directly or indirectly, of the use and application of any of the contents of this work.

Table Of Contents

Praise For The Book

'Born To Stand Out, Not To Fit In, *is a very captivating, empowering, emotional and easy to read book. This is a true account of the ordeal the author encountered who I happen to be honoured to be close to. Teuta is a very powerful woman of God and a spiritual leader too. The book has clearly demonstrated this aspect of her including her strong faith and belief in God. All these helped her in her miraculous escape from unimaginable situations. This highly inspirational book is worth investing in."*
Nicky Oke, Property Investor, BA (Hons) Econs., MBA, DBA Researcher, DWP/Kings College, Cambridge University Summer School Graduate, Co-founder Niam Assets LTD, www.NiamAssets.com

"This book is a source of inspiration to everyone that is going through adversity of any sort. It proves that, it doesn't matter whatever challenge you are experiencing, the power to overcome it lies within us. This is definitely an interesting read and I will encourage everyone to read this book for we all are bound to experience one form of challenge or the other at different stages of our life. Thanks Teuta for inspiring the world by sharing your own story so that we can all learn from it."
Aminu Ahmadu, Property Investor, Co-founder Niam

Assets LTD., www.NiamAssets.com

"Teuta Avdyli's thoughtful, heartfelt and captivating story takes the reader on a journey of heroic proportions. She is an inspiration to be unshakable in the face of adversity. As a motivational speaker, I was moved by her examples of mindfulness, forgiveness and empowering belief in positive prayers. This book is pleasing to read for anyone wanting to move beyond their current existence and find a meaningful purpose to their lives."
Jaina Ford, CEO of X2Cme LLC, Public Speaker, Narrator and Producer, www.x2cme.com

"Teuta's book is an embodiment of practical tools, strategies and prayers that break old patterns. It speaks life and truth to humanity and allows us to focus on what is important now."
Adaobi Onyekweli, Author of the book "Reinvent Yourself"

"I am a survivor myself and as a psychotherapist / mentor I have worked deeply in healing the losses and the grief of many people. I could see since I met Teuta how she has risen over her difficulties and challenges in life and is now at

service to humanity with a smile in her face and a steady heartbeat which allows her to be fully present for her clients, friends & family. She is indeed an extraordinary woman and you can see it as you go through reading this wonderful book."

Viola Edward, Author, TransCultural Psychotherapist & Breathwork Lead Trainer
www.ViolaEdward.com

"Teuta is one of the most inspirational people I know. She has travelled an incredible journey of hope, of courage and triumphed through a true testing of the strength of the human spirit. God has blessed Teuta and her amazing passion and her wisdom is collected within the pages of this book. It's a must read for anyone who is searching for their soul purpose or a road map towards the life that you truly deserve.

Teuta's techniques take you to the core of your being, and through self-empowerment & life-skills towards the greatest potential within. "Born To Stand Out, Not To Fit In" will inspire you to take your next level in life, and the results that you will achieve will be extraordinary!"

Steve Frew, Scotland's First Gymnastics Commonwealth Games Gold Medallist
www.SteveFrew.co.uk

Foreword By Harry Sardinas
Public Speaking, Empowerment and Leadership Coach

Teuta Avdyli is an inspirational, courageous young woman who has inspired me and many other people to achieve more beyond our expectations. She has gone through horrific situations only to come out of them empowered spiritually.

I met Teuta when she came to my Speakers Are Leaders public speaking and branding course. As an empowerment, public speaking and leadership trainer, I was astonished to see the drive, enthusiasm, passion and inspiration she spoke with.

There are not so many women in the world who can hold an audience's attention like Teuta can, because the experiences she has gone through have made her even more powerful and exciting as a person and speaker.

Teuta has survived against all odds, coming to the UK as a refugee, escaping life-threatening situations, a terrible lorry accident and ongoing immigration issues.

Many times in life, when people tell you that you can't do something, oftentimes, you may struggle to try again multiple times. Teuta has become an even bigger fighter and for that reason, I have no doubt she will inspire thousands of people with her message.

She can empower you spiritually, she can motivate you with positive language, encouragement and emotional support.

The future is looking very bright for Teuta and I highly recommend you read this magical book she arduously wrote in order to inspire you to achieve anything you want without limitations.

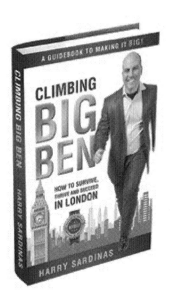 

Note To The Reader

Dear Reader,

Think about the last time you felt ALIVE. When I say "alive", I really mean full of life, full of excitement. When was the last time you felt excited about living? When was the last time you felt you could not wait to wake up in the morning, because you love your life?

I feel like this every single day. I am grateful, I am contented, I feel enthusiastic about everything I am doing because I absolutely adore my life the way it is. There is no questioning the fact that it is possible, because I want progress and growth.

I am rejoicing every single minute and I want to show you how you can feel that every day, too.
Read on, and I hope one day you will write to me about how your life has transformed.

Acknowledgements

Writing a book about the story of your life is a surreal process and it is more rewarding than I could have ever imagined.

First and foremost, I would like to give glory to God that I am alive and I am being of use. I would like to thank the Almighty for giving me the strength, wisdom, ability and opportunity to undertake, persevere and complete the book. Without His direction, this achievement would not have been possible.

He made all the things possible for me until the end. I have a legacy to pass on to my family and beyond, where one didn't exist before.

I have to start by thanking my awesome family – my husband, and my children, Helena and Daniel – who read early drafts and gave me advice on the book cover, pictures, and shared their wonderful ideas and thoughts. I love you, my precious stones!

Thank you especially to my sister, Rezarta, for always being there for me when I needed her support and help with the children, doing school runs and cooking.

I am also eternally grateful to my husband's niece, Naze Haskja who put in extra time to help me with the children, feeding them and putting them to bed when I was at late evening meetings. She didn't have to. Thank you, Naze.

I'm forever indebted to Lily Patrascu and Harry Sardinas for their keen insight and ongoing support in bringing my stories to life in this book, and for helping me and other authors to turn our ideas into stories and published books. None of this would have been possible without their help.

Thank you to Harry Sardinas for training me to become a public speaker with the Speakers Are Leaders speaking, marketing and branding programme. Thanks to the publishing team.

I would like to thank Nicky Oke, my valuable friend, who said to me: "You have to write your own book, my dear," for her professional guidance and valuable support, and her useful and constructive recommendations. Thank you, Nicky.

Thank you to Bishop Alvaro Lima, for his prayers and valuable advice. Also to my spiritual true friend, Samantha Dixon, who's been my witness, and has seen what I have overcome over the years.

To all of those who have been part of my getting there, who have helped me with the book, even with one idea, one word, one direction, to all I am very grateful indeed. God bless you all!
Thank you...I am honoured and thankful to be part of the Entrepreneur Mastermind Team!

And last, but not least, I want to thank UCKG Help Centre – the place where I grew and matured spiritually over the years. I truly have no idea where I'd be if I hadn't been spiritually strong. UCKG Help Centre was like a roof over my head when I desperately needed it, in times of struggle, and was where I learnt how to live by faith.

About The Book

Born To Stand Out, Not To Fit In. Empower Yourself To Live An Extraordinary Life is the ultimate guide for you to empower yourself to achieve your goals and dreams by becoming spiritually awakened and balanced. It is based on the Empowerment Mastery System that Teuta created to inspire you become more productive, more driven, and more alive. It will help you find your purpose in life and activate your full potential.

My Story

Imagine a healthy, active, pretty young woman. It really felt like I had absolutely nothing to worry about. I was sporty, healthy, full of energy, and married with two beautiful children. What more could I possibly desire? At times, I thought I was pursuing my purpose in my life, but then I would get distracted.

I often found myself pondering a deeper meaning to my existence – what exactly was my real purpose in life? Deep down inside of me, since I was a young girl, I always believed that there was something greater waiting for me, and I was searching to find that right thing.

What could it be? In the background of my constant activities, there was this small voice that I had seemed to ignore and kept it to myself. "Is this all?" I often wondered, as I monotonously lived my days. Although I lived with a lot of passion, whatever thing I did was with respect and reverence.

I was always doing my best, always having goals, improving, growing, involving hobbies. I realised I was stuck in a default survival mode. Little did I know something terrible was going to happen that would change my life forever!

About Me

How I embraced my new life in the UK!

I came to the UK in late 2000 as a refugee from the Albanian territory. The whole transition of coming to the UK wasn't a smooth one. We passed the border on a small boat and were thrown into the deep sea and left fighting for our lives.

The owner of the boat threw everyone into the deep water, as they were chased by a guardian helicopter. They wanted to save their own lives and zoomed fast to get out from the patrolled zone, and left everyone in God's hope. I screamed for help and waved frantically at my husband because I was terrified.

I didn't know how to swim, and my mouth was full of water. I was desperate for air. When it really struck me that I was about to drown, I experienced an acute sense of loneliness and isolation, as another wave thrust me down. I swallowed water and tried not to breathe it in.

In that moment of despair, I realised that someone had brought me up from the depths of the water. I recognised my husband's voice, telling me: "I got you, I won't let you die, you're safe now," and he managed to pull me all the way to the seashore.

After an extremely risky experience, we managed to make our way to Belgium and, finally, we arrived in the UK!
Moving to a new country, I faced challenge after challenge. I didn't know what was ahead of me in this new big country. Language was a barrier and a difficult task to conquer.

It was a new life that was different from the one I left behind. I had to adapt to new places, a new culture, a new way of eating and living – I had a completely new world to discover. It was a life-changing experience that was very different from where I grew up.

It was all about exploration and adaptation. You get to know so many things in so little time. I remember I asked myself this vital question, "Am I creating a life here?" The fear I felt from the unknown as a foreigner was beyond my comfort zone.

I had to gain a sense of courage and allow myself to have a wide variety of experiences. I had to learn the process of adjustments, emotions, and to achieve the "impossible". I had to embrace my life as an expat. It was my responsibility, only mine, to accept, embrace, and learn.

There have been many struggles on my way, which I had to overcome. I was young and inexperienced to deal with all the uncertainty that was to come. I lived with my husband in an emergency accommodation for seven months, and after that we were moved to eight temporary accommodations. I didn't have a place to call a home for a very long time.

We also faced long years of immigration problems, which meant I lost so many opportunities. However, despite these hindrances, I managed the best I could. After sixteen years of waiting, we were granted Leave to Remain (LR) and, finally, in 2017, I got my British Citizen Passport.

That was a long battle to fight, and a good one to win. While waiting nervously and solving other matters, I found comfort and fulfilment in supplementing and investing in my education, and enhanced my personal and professional skills.

I started meeting new people and joined expat communities. Also, making new friends from different cultures and backgrounds was a major learning experience and very rewarding indeed. I continued growing academically, year after year.

I finished all levels in computing with distinction, achieved a Foundation degree, and gained an Honours degree in Computer Science, with high grades, in 2008. I also finished Teaching Assistant Levels 2 and 3. I know that nothing is impossible if you have the right desire and determination.

The unique experience I went through, creating a home here, has enriched my life. It showed me I was capable of achieving and accomplishing anything if I only put my mind to it. It showed me how strong I was and how I could overcome pretty much everything I set my mind to.

Most importantly, I have known myself along the way and the reward is quite enormous! The tests you face in your life are not to reveal your weaknesses but to help you discover your inner strengths. You can only know how strong you are when you strive and thrive beyond those challenges.

I don't want to sound too cocky, but I do consider myself an empowered woman. My point is, you shouldn't be reluctant to take steps in life. If you have fears, you will definitely suffer. When you take risks, you will learn that there will be times when you fail, there will be times when you succeed, but they are both equally important.

Failure is part of the process to succeed, and it's the necessary stepping stone to achieving your dreams. Live your life to the fullest, live the moment, and enjoy the power of the present, because everything else is uncertain. If something goes wrong, here is my advice ...

If I could overcome all I have been through, and believe me there were many challenges, I don't have any doubt whatsoever that you can, too – no matter what situation you are in. I managed to KEEP CALM, CARRY ON, AND PUSH THROUGH.

I learnt so much over the years, since I had to do so much bouncing back, and I became a quick learner to get on with it. I think these challenges are a powerful sustainer of accountability and they allow you to discover your inner strengths.

The biggest lesson I learnt was to smash my own spiders and get on with my day. In three words, LIFE GOES ON, whether you decide to stay stuck or move forward! It's Your Choice, Your Decision, and Your Life! Whatever choice you make, it determines who you become. So, choose wisely.

My Turning Point

You are conditioned to believe that your life revolves around great moments, which also means a wealth of experience. Everyone will experience adversity at some point in life, but you can overcome it with the right attitude, which is the necessary component to do exceedingly well. Overcome and prevail.

But, your great moments often catch you unaware, unprepared and surprised. You may feel a change is going to happen, but you just don't know what that change is or what form or capacity it might take. It's that moment when you say; "I can't take it anymore, I have reached my limits."

That moment against the "impossible", when you say, "That's it, I am done." But here's the thing ...
Herodotus, the Greek philosopher, said, "Adversity has the effect of drawing out strength and qualities of a man that

would have lain dormant in its absence."

1. The Accident

I was feeling happy about my life in general. Finally, my kids were full-time at school and I was rejoicing that I had time to do my own thing; to finish my Master's degree, that's what I thought ... That Wednesday morning I was enjoying my bicycle ride on that breezy, beautiful, sunny day.

I stopped at the traffic lights where I was waiting, when out of blue I was knocked down on the ground (how quick an accident can occur!) on the side of the road. I couldn't comprehend what was happening to me. A big heavy goods lorry (God knows how many tons of weight) rode over my poor legs.

At that point, I began screaming, but the driver didn't see me. And again, another ran over my legs. I knew I was set for an impact and in this moment, I didn't know if I'd live or die – there was pure terror. I saw a steel pole in front of me and I grabbed it with my two hands, so I could drag myself out of the way.

I hoped to save my leg from another roll over. But I couldn't – my feet were stuck and trapped in the bicycle wheels. I felt utterly powerless, overwhelmed, and helpless. I screamed for help with an exceedingly great and bitter cry. I remember the feeling of complete acceptance of death.

Suddenly, a lady got the driver's attention. Though the shock of the impact was so intense that there was nothing I could have done to adequately overcome it. I raised my head to look at the state of my leg – I saw a pool of blood! At this point, I was panicking as I realised something was severely wrong.

In that very moment, I lifted up my voice and wept. I also raised my eyes on to the clear, beautiful sky and said:

"God ... please .. let me live! You are my only and last hope ... Forgive me, please. I have belittled You when you hold it all, king of the world. Let me live – even if it is without legs! I may not have legs, but please keep my mind and make me strong. Don't let my children grow without their mum, do not let them become orphans."

While I was lying down on the ground, this woman stayed with me the whole time – God bless her! I said to her, "I am hurt badly, I will not be able to walk again."

"Shhh … just breathe, please," she said quietly. "You're going to be fine."

She looked at me again like she read my mind and I looked at her, waiting for an answer from her. "Yes, you're a bit hurt, but you will get help in no time," she said. She continued applying pressure to my leg. The lorry driver came to me, his face looking pale.

I felt sorry for him, too. "How come you didn't see me? How come you …?" I kept asking him, but he was silent, there were no spoken words. Silence … Just me sighing from the intense pain.

2. The Ambulance

The emergency services – the police and the ambulance – arrived after what seemed like an endless wait. The agony was like white noise. The police got my phone and asked what the password was. I couldn't answer, I couldn't articulate any words, I was tongue-tied.

Everything was like a white cloud. Just intense pain. I felt deep inside that I was leaving. Tears were rolling down my cheeks, and in that moment I fell in love with life and wanted to live. At this point, I thought of my children. "No, I have to live!" I was battling with two inner voices.

I didn't want to accept the endless negative thoughts that were bombarding my mind. I had to push through the walls and I started to pray without ceasing. That wasn't any kind of prayer, but a deep outcry, desperate, and a different kind of prayer, for sure.

I had my faith and it was everything I needed. Suddenly, something opened up deep inside me, and I could sense someone's presence on my left shoulder. I wasn't alone, for sure. The sense of peace and an unbelievable strength came over me. I remember vividly that pivotal moment.

I gave a long, very loud scream and a piercing cry mixed with extreme emotion and unbearing pain. "Love!" I yelled the password of my phone. "Well done." The police comforted me. No one answered the phone, no husband, no friends.

"My children, my children, they are at school," I murmured.

"Don't worry, someone will go and look after them," said one of the policemen.

"Please pray for me!" I said, and immediately I was surrounded by prayers. God bless them all.

I felt warm and peaceful. Know this; there is no past, there is no future, only the present moment exists. Nothing mattered anymore. No worries, no memories, no family, and no loved ones; in fact, nothing entered into my mind in that moment.

It seemed like I was floating on the bright shining sky. I could feel that presence. I was still breathing and hoping to take in another breath and another one after that. I never knew up to that moment how precious the air that I breathed was and how precious life was, too!

If I could capture that feeling and sell it, I'd be a billionaire. But ... I can't. I don't have the capacity to describe it, none of us has, and nothing can be put into words to articulate it. It's beyond any human understanding. I could feel that sensation, energy, vibration, through every fibre of my body.

I could feel it, and it was the most wonderful thing, the energy of my own soul. Being heart-led, I was thinking less and feeling more. I decluttered my mind and could hear the sound of my inner voice talking. Whenever you find yourself in tough situations, always trust that voice, because it is your built-in sensor of your divinity.

My own soul was in a deep connection with the beauty of the universe. What an amazing feeling! I had a deep connection with the source itself. I knew that there was something greater than myself, which I was a part of, and the greatness was a part of me.

Right there were my defining moments! I would not change them for anything in the world. That was my life-changing experience. I simply knew that I was right where I was meant to be. Trust your journey! How foolish we humans are that we take life for granted.

We give up our power too easily to people, places, situations and circumstances. Most especially, we worry about the little and petty things. I was guilty of that; I worried about my children's clubs, schools, and tuition fee. I used to send them everywhere – kung fu, piano, ballet, dancing, football, swimming, etc.

I became aware of that, but we are so busy that we lose ourselves in the tangible and material aspects of life. We get distracted and we don't often hear the soft whispering voice of our own soul, calling and giving us signals and messages about what we are supposed to be doing.

When I think of that moment, long after the accident, I still become breathless. That moment captivated and resonated in me and will stay with me for as long as I live. Every time I see my leg (it's a big scar, not pleasant to look at, but I love it), it reminds me how much God loves me, and also of that moment! The scar tells a story. A story of my testimony!

My advice: You don't have to go through what I experienced just to appreciate and start living life to the fullest. There should be no wasting of time. No ugly clothes. No boring movies. No negative people. I was saved to escape that deadly accident, and God gave me a second chance.

How about you? You never know if you'll have a second chance, we don't know what the future holds. We just breathe and the rest is unknown. I learnt my lesson, a very valuable one. The good thing is that we have a choice on how to live our lives, we can either make or break by our own choices.

My "If" statements to help you:

- If I love openly, then I will be loved.
- If I have money, then I will serve others.
- If I take challenges, then I will make my dreams happen.
- If I tell myself positive things daily, then good things will happen.
- If I live in the moment, then I will be grateful for little things.
- If I invest, the money will grow.
- If I focus on my dreams, then it will happen.
- If I stop wasting my time, then I will invest in myself.
- If I am not afraid of succeeding, then I will greatly perform.
- If I know my purpose, then I will leave a legacy.

My point: Our life is not measured by how many breaths we take, but by the Moments that take our ... Breath ... Away. When I think of that Moment, I always become ... Breathless!

3. In The Hospital

I was rushed to the Accident & Emergency department at the Royal London Hospital. I managed to gulp down the gas and air in the ambulance – it seemed to be a long journey, as I was in intense pain. I went straight to the operating theatre for a wound wash. I don't remember anything after that until I opened my eyes, woken by the voice of my husband calling me.

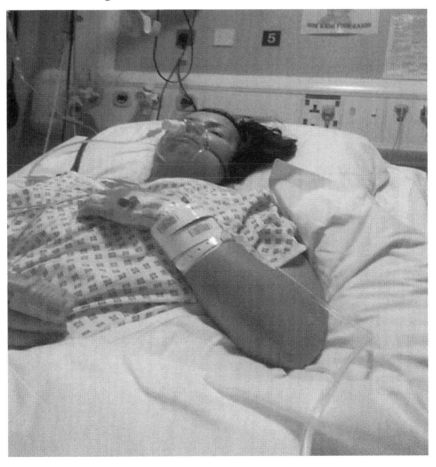

When I opened my eyes, I was happy that I was alive.

I had undergone two major operations and three wound washes, all under anaesthetic. Bone was taken from my hip, and skin from my left leg then my right thigh, as the first skin graft didn't sit properly. The last skin for the graft was taken from my right leg.

I remember as I was wheeled down the corridor to the operating room for my main operation. I was a peace that surpassed any understanding. I knew that I was going to be alright. The main operation lasted for twelve hours. I remember looking at the time when I was getting prepared for the operation: 9.17 a.m., and I woke up at 9.30 p.m.

My family cried like I was dead because they never imagined that I would come out from that surgery theatre door alive, after all of that waiting in agony and exhaustion. In fact, I had to give them strength and assured them that I was going to be fine.

I used to say to them, "You should celebrate that I am alive." After those long hours of surgery, I was rushed again to the theatre the next day, as the skin graft didn't sit. I was in hospital for one month. I will never forget what my doctor said to me the next day he saw me.

He said, "You know that you had a very terrible and nasty accident. I want to say that your leg will never be the same again." Tears rolled down from my eyes; tears of mixed feelings, but of joy, too. I thought he was going to say that he had to amputate my leg, but instead he said, "You're very lucky that you're alive.

I don't even know how you have your foot attached to your leg." The truth is, I knew that I wasn't lucky because I don't believe in luck – instead, I believe in blessing. I believe in miracles and I am glad that I am here! I was being prepared to meet the opportunity, to do things differently this time.

I feel no resentment and no anger against anything. Instead, I thank God that I am alive that I am above the ground and not underneath. Now, I am glad and I know the answers to my "whats": ***"What should I do with my life?" "What is my passion?"*** or ***"What is my life purpose?" "What's my identity?"***

I really believe God fuelled me with a great meaning and purpose.

4. Home Recovery

The accident left me bedridden and immobilised for eight months, and my family was put into a difficult situation. I had to learn to walk again, like a baby. One day, after seeing the results of the X-ray, my doctor didn't look too happy. He was concerned that the bone taken from my hip hadn't knitted together with the other ankle bone.

He gave me an appointment to see him soon. I was concerned and asked him questions. "Of course, if the bone doesn't knit properly, there will be other complications," he said. Before the day of the appointment, at around three in the morning, I was woken up and I prayed.

As I closed my eyes, a breathtaking and miraculous thing happened. With my eyes closed, I saw the most beautiful picture that I could ever imagine or describe. It was so perfectly made; the colours and the image itself. I saw two big hands holding a leg and it was spinning very slowly all around.

Obviously, I was shocked, and scared, too. I didn't know what was going on! Then, the image went away. Then, another picture of an ankle was formed, swirling around very slowly, and I could see it in every detail. What an incredible image.

That beauty went away and bright clouds appeared. In that moment, I opened my eyes as I couldn't take it anymore, or maybe that was it. I was covered in tears and couldn't comprehend what had just happened! I was breathless! That day, I went to see my doctor.

I had an X-ray taken, and was waiting for him to see me. The nurse called my name. I could see the doctor from the corridor, he was smiling at me and he said, "Teuta, I don't have any concerns anymore. The bone has knitted together very well."

Can you picture my joy and excitement in that moment? I thought of the vision I saw earlier that morning and it made perfect sense. God answered my prayer through that vision of "that beautiful ankle". Wow, what an experience! I felt for sure privileged.

It has been over two years since then, and I am still struggling daily. I had to undergo months of physiotherapy and hydrotherapy to help my damaged ankle, nerve, and muscle, but nothing could rebuild my attitude to cycling again – the thrill of being at one with nature.

I experience sadness when I think I can't cycle anymore, which was something that I enjoyed so much. That day had been the last enjoyable bicycle ride of my life and my hobby simply died, but a new chapter has opened up in my life!
I couldn't have come so far alone, I couldn't have done it without help from God and my family.

You can't survive in this world just by believing in yourself. You're not big enough. I am not big enough to do it, no one is. It has been a unique experience for my children, too. Watching me overcome my struggles made them understand that life isn't always easy.

I remember them not being afraid to look at my wound. I will never forget when my son, Daniel, who was five years old at that time, was praying every night:
"My God, please, please make my mum's leg the same as the other leg."

He would come straight to my bed every morning when he woke up and look at my leg and say: "Oh, Mummy, your leg is getting better. Thank you, God, You're answering my prayer." How heartwarming ... seeing his eyes full of hope and hearing his innocent words left me gobsmacked. "Mummy, you smell like a hooospital."

He was stretching, lengthening the word "hospital". "But don't worry, Mummy, you soon will smell like a flower again, very soon." He made me laugh so much and that made me forget all the pain. My daughter, Helena, eight years old, used to massage my foot every time and looked after me.

The time of my recovery was long and I am still recovering, but I wouldn't change it for anything. I had my quiet moments to reflect over my life. I look at things with much sensitivity, now. I knew that I was saved for a reason. I knew that my time here on Earth hadn't finished yet.

I knew that I was prepared for a greater impact. I knew something had to change. God is my strength, my refuge, and in Him I trust! I know that I am an earthly vessel, but greater is He who was and is in me, shines brighter than any star in the midst of my tribulation, adversity, and darkest moments.

I remember asking this question, which became part of my everyday life: "My God, please help me understand my purpose on Earth. Who am I? Help me to see things through Your eyes. Let me think like You, and let me love like You do. I know that You didn't throw me on Earth unintentionally."

The more I prayed, the clearer my identity became, and the more I understood who I truly was. I was in the process of refining, pruning, and restoration. You have to see the gap between where you are now and where you want to be, and be aware of that gap, which is one's first objective – to take some time to know ourselves.

Otherwise, if you don't know who you are, you will certainly feel lost. I had my moments of reflection and listening time with greatest source. Nothing had been a waste. God's timing is perfect, He's never too late, never too early, but just in time.

I started to listen more to my inner voice, so I would know what I needed to change in me. One of the messages was, "Slow down and take it easy. You are worrying too much, you can't do anything by worrying. Remove your worries and just trust me."

That opened my eyes to have unshakable trust. It also made me realise how important it was not only to pray, but also to listen to what God has to say to us.

We can transform someone's life with our words rather than causal intention.

Chapter 1
Empowerment Starts With You

How To Empower Yourself

1. Getting Started with Self-Empowerment:

There is only one kind of empowerment, and that is self-empowerment. Unlike granting authority, empowerment comes from within. By empowering yourself, you take the actions and the risks to achieve a result and get what you want.

Empowerment is not to be confused with superiority. They are two totally different things. To be empowered means to be strong, confident, making the most out of each situation, as a preparation to meet the opportunity, especially in controlling your life and claiming your rights.

You don't wait for someone to declare you empowered, rather you step outside your comfort zone, and make things happen. It takes a plan and a support system. This how-to guide is full of wisdom, top tips, and exercises to inspire an old dream or create a new one, in order to expand your innate intelligence and take action toward your dreams and ambitions.

You become mature when you stop complaining, and start making changes, and when you are sufficiently informed and knowledgeable to make better decisions. I believe perspective is often the biggest difference between struggle and success. If we can change perspective, we can change the story and we can change the outcome.

Reconnect with your dreams and start your personal transformation with the new inspirational book, *Born to Stand Out, Not To Fit In*.

The Empowerment Mastery System

12 Things You Need To Know
To Empower And Make A Powerful Impact On People
By Engaging Every Aspect Of Their Being

Empowerment is a process that I have come to condense into the Empowerment Mastery System – a process which, once implemented, will start to yield positive results. The Empowerment Mastery System contains twelve steps which, combined together, will lead to a life full of love and fun, which will feel like it is what you were meant to do on Earth.

It will help you become a better version of you. Regularly follow through with these and you'll be well on your way to living your extraordinary life.

These steps are shown below and thoroughly explained in the upcoming chapters:

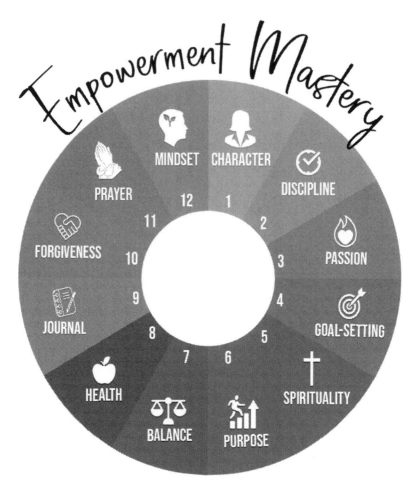

1. Character   2. Discipline

3. Passion   4. Goal-setting

5. Spirituality   6. Purpose

7. Balance   8. Health

9. Journal   10. Forgiveness

11. Prayer   12. Mindset

EMPOWERING

Is About Helping And Serving Others To Reach Their Potential.

- ## Learn Strong Character Traits

What Is Good Character?

When a person possesses good character it can be observed through their actions. It's not limited to a single value, but the traits are demonstrated in the "good" choices they make and the "bad" choices they avoid. So, how do you begin to improve your character?

1. Be Confident – Speak out and let your voice be heard. Stand up for others. Lead by example. Turn your dreams into useful plans. A confident woman is easy to spot. She respects herself in everything she does. She is significant in every way: the way she dresses, the way she walks, the way she thinks, and the way she talks. Be that woman.

2. Be A Pleasing Personality – Your personality consists of the sum of your mental and physical traits, which distinguish you from all other people, and which determine whether you are liked or disliked. I would like to share five important points at which people contact you and evaluate your personality, whether you recognise it or not.

The first point is a *smile personality*. When you think about it, a **smile** means so many things. It can convey confidence, happiness, and even approval. People, as a whole, look for someone else to **smile** because it makes them feel good inside.

There is an old saying that when you smile, the whole world smiles back at you. People love to see someone smile because it conveys happiness. A smile makes people believe that you are confident in what you are saying and believe in what you are doing.

The second point is *presenting yourself*. People evaluate you just by the way you look to them, or how you present yourself or even what clothes you wear. I don't know whether that's 100% true, but I know one thing for sure – that the first impression matters. First Impressions Are Often Lasting Impressions.

The third point is *listening skills.* People with pleasing personalities tend to be good listeners and conversationalists. They handle situations well and share their opinion in an agreeable manner.

The fourth point is your *presence.* People evaluate your personality according to how they feel when they are close to you. You should aim to make them feel good about themselves. You meet their values, and empower them in the area that they are disempowered.

You just know that being in the presence of people with pleasing personalities is good, even without them saying anything. You should keep a positive point of view and demonstrate flexibility and patience.

The fifth point is that people with pleasing personalities typically *like people and interacting with others.* They treat people fairly and with so much respect.

3. *Speak Openly* — When you speak openly, you show your opinion without any fear and without hiding your character.

4. Be Unabashedly Passionate — Become led by passion, passion for work, passion for life, passion for yourself, passion for everything. A woman that is dedicated with passion is loved without any hesitation. They have passion and it is genuine.

5. Be Honest — This is a very important trait of someone's character. Everyone likes women that are honest and brave. Women that show fear and cover the truth to protect themselves by lying are not desirable ...

Character
Produces
HOPE

- **Have High Standards**

Lowering your standards is never worth it – never. You don't have to settle for someone just because you're alone and you want to find love. Surely, we all deserve to be loved, respected, and treated nicely, but when we don't get it from others, we have to have it for ourselves.

Unless you expect far more from your romantic partners – then you're on the right path. If you feel that they are not good enough, then don't date them. You need to date someone who isn't an afterthought. Don't be amazed or deceived by their look, or their big muscles. You never know one day if he may use those muscles against you.

Don't just settle for a warm body across the dinner table, but a man that has a positive connection. Have standards and stick with them, you deserve it and you are worthy!
Here are six steps to keep your expectations high and attain anything you desire:

1. Understand What You Want And Be Goal-Orientated.

"A busy, vibrant, goal-oriented woman is so much more attractive than a woman who waits around for a man to validate her existence." Mandy Hale.

When you know what you want, you come to know that you are worth more and deserve the best for your life.

Don't settle for anything less than exactly what you want! Respect yourself and never compare your life, your standards, or your norms with others just to get to your desired destination. Be open to receive others' opinion and advice, and do not be afraid to ask for help.

Actually, lowering your standards practically dooms you to unhappiness. This is especially true if you've always known what you want. You know that you don't deserve to live beneath a dark cloud, especially since the person with lower standards is simply not your match!

2. The Love Of Your Life Is You.

Why look outside yourself for something that is already within you? True love starts within you. The love of your life is nobody else but you. Within you lies all the love that you need and desire. In you, and not outside of you. The love you will receive from outside of yourself will be nothing but a projection of the love that is present within you.

3. Think Big And Never Say: "Am I Asking For Too Much?" Instead Focus On: "I Deserve It"

Sometimes we think "too small". Let's start thinking bigger, and see what happens. The magic of possibility lies in the unknown. Realise that we are part of the whole world and believe in your inherent purpose. Have you ever thought that the idea you have in your mind could have the capacity to change the world in some way, or at the very least change you?

Follow your heart's desire or dreams and stretch out your thoughts. Realise your greatest potential. Embrace your place among the many. You are a valuable piece in the universal puzzle!

4. Work Hard And Be At The Top Of The Game.

Empowered people always seek ways to grow personally and professionally. Even when you're at your peak, focus only on getting better. Work hard to get to where you want to be.

Love the sound of your feet walking away from things that are not meant for you – learn, grow, evolve, and don't show any signs of stopping.

You don't need to climb down from your top spot, just because no one else can hang with you.

5. If Someone Wants You, They Have To Climb With You.

Choose a partner who is not only proud to be with you, but will also take every risk just to be with you. You want to be with someone who is ambitious and focused on constantly bettering themselves in every facet of life. Why should you have to climb down to meet someone who is unwilling to put in the effort to join you at the top?
What you will allow is what will continue ...

6. If You Respect Yourself And Your Standards, Others Will, Too.

Raising your standards will take you to a higher level in life. Refuse to disrespect yourself by lowering or shrinking your standards just to make others feel comfortable or to fit in. They might not agree and they might not fit your standards, but they'll respect that you have them, of course.

DEMAND THE BEST FOR YOURSELF.

Aim High.
You're Worth It.
You Have The Right.

- ## Be Passionate And Significant

You feel very powerful when you do what you love. That, right there, is empowerment to me. Make the most of each opportunity presented to you and live your dreams to the fullest! There is no better time than the present.

I love one quote by R.S. Grey:

"She believed she could, so she did."

It's so simple, but it delivers a very powerful message – you can do anything if you put your mind to it. Nothing is impossible – in fact, the word itself says: "I'm possible". Every single person has a voice and an opinion that deserves to be heard.

When the world becomes silent, even one voice becomes powerful, and it can change the world. Don't let anyone tell you that you can't. Never believe that. It's just a fat lie.

There is no doubt that I am a woman in process, and I've learned from every conflict and every experience.

In the end, some of your greatest pains become your greatest strengths. You become a better version of yourself: the way you think, the way you speak, the way you perceive things, and the way you project the future is completely different when you have a difficult experience.

Every Tear That
Comes Out From
Your Eyes Is Just To
Plant Your Seeds
For The Best Fruit.

- ## Improve And Unlock Your Full Potential

Learn from the mistakes that you make. You will know the way next time by not going on the same path, and taking a different route. It's more like a GPS that says you're two minutes away from your destination, but all of a sudden it says "rerouting" – which means to take a different direction to reach your destination.

Never give up on your dreams – keep going until you achieve it, no matter what it takes, and no matter how long it will take. When you fail, get back up and try again, it's just a feedback to take the next step to success.

LEARN FROM YOUR MISTAKES,

They Are Just Feedback For Starting Again.

• **Be So Good That They Can't Ignore You**

There will always be someone – a friend, or even a family member – that will put you down with their words at some point. "You can't do this," or "You can't do that." "Who do you think you are?" or "You're not good enough." "It's impossible," or "It's hard," etc.

I think the best thing to do is to give them the silent treatment, meaning that you don't get involved to persuade them. Note: don't confuse silence with acceptance. Do not go down to their level; instead, concentrate on your dreams, prove them wrong by doing very well.

I am convinced that this is the best sweet "revenge", when you succeed and prove them wrong. Be so good that they can't ignore your outcome. Succeed and do a fantastic job at whatever you're called to do. And remember, life is a marathon and not a sprint. Be a turtle.

I am sure there is no better answer to that. Actions speak louder than words.

A More Positive, Peaceful, Grateful State Of Being Shows Up As The

BEST

VERSION OF

YOU.

• Work On Your Self-Awareness

Throughout our life we discover what we are good at, and what we love to do. Your vision will become so clear to you when you look into your own heart.

C.G. Jung said it very well: "Who looks outside, dreams; who looks inside, awakes."

Figure out what your gifts are and work on the enlightenment of your personality and character and, once you have figured it out, follow that belief and be committed. Have the determination and never give up on your dreams. I didn't give up; instead, I turned my story around in order to empower others.

There are two ways to live: you can live as if nothing is a miracle or you can live as if everything is a miracle. I want to use my miracle and experience to raise awareness of how precious life is. That moment "awakened" me to understand my life here on Earth whilst I am alive, right now! No more procrastination.

I want to be useful and leave a legacy behind!

You Have A Story Inside Of You Waiting To Be Written.
Just Give Yourself Permission.

Break Your Silence And Suffering.

• Embrace Your Life And Expect Change

The good thing is, we decide what is positive or negative – the circumstance has not changed – but how we perceive and subsequently respond to it has practically changed. Perceptions that paint a viewpoint of negativity can draw back the power to you, rather than your situation.

See the beauty and understand both the pain and the joy that exist in life as an experience. Moving through difficult circumstances enhances that inner power – and it all begins with believing in yourself. It's not the situation, but how we respond and react to the situation – negative or positive – that matters.

By following your heart, you essentially invite into your life meaningful occurrences that may appear to be a coincidence. I believe that there are no coincidences. The creation of the universe works in a rhythmic pattern, through waves of energy and connection.

When you pay attention to these meaningful occurrences, they naturally increase in frequency. These little messages that you note down or recall with some vital significance can simply let you know that you are right where you are meant to be.

Live
Like You're Dying Today And

LEARN

Like You're Living Forever.

•   **Knowledge Is Power. Act Upon It!**

Knowledge is power, but if you don't act upon it, that idea or knowledge becomes unused. The only thing that makes us powerless in our life is the lack of proper knowledge about life. Knowing how to handle difficult situations in times of struggle is what makes us or breaks us to be the winners and leaders of our life.

Having the ability to create powerful understanding in times of crisis is the definition of someone who is a leader of their life. Knowledge serves like a weapon that is meant to protect you from breaking down in times of hardship. Having the right knowledge weapons is very essential in order to be the winner of your life.

Strive for the right knowledge about life to be able to create powerful interpretations of situations in your life.

To overcome and become more self-empowered you must invest so much in yourself, enhance your self-determination, and build your character. Gather knowledge about the situation and possible methods of handling it. Be well-resourced.

Know yourself, what is appropriate for you, and take full responsibility for your thoughts, feelings, and behaviour.

Everything we are and everything we've achieved is because of our ability to learn and to act upon it – otherwise it's useless.

People who go on a high level are nothing more than extremely efficient. They implement efficiency in their areas of focus. If you do, you'll overcome whatever obstacles are thrown in your path and be able to build the life you've always wanted to have!

Self-empowerment is not something that is handed to you, rather it's something you give to yourself as a gift. It means taking complete control of your own life.

Be Simple And Authentic.

Don't Change Because You Want To Please Others.

• **Be Authentic**

Be yourself. Take care to exercise your own ideas, your free will and independence. Live from your individual uniqueness and the willingness to be different from others. Your authenticity is that place within you that is true. When you are true to yourself and passionate about your life, you choose to see choice rather than challenge.

Your true essence is not set up on false pretences, because whatever path you choose in life, personal and professional, is completely congruent with who you are. There is no one like you. God doesn't love us equally, rather He loves us uniquely. Each of us is authentic, and none of us has the same DNA or fingerprint. We are each a masterpiece.

Beauty comes from within. You have to keep your mind, soul, body, and spirit in sync. I am a firm and strong believer that when you are happy, feel joy and love, you radiate beauty from the inside, out.
You are released from shackles, chains, or other physical restraints.

The Privilege Of A Lifetime Is To

BECOME WHO YOU TRULY ARE.

Chapter 2
How To Overcome Difficult Situations And Discipline Yourself To Have A Successful Life

We all want to live a simple and a happy life, a life that is far away from negative thoughts and a life of action. But there are many obstacles in our way. Our mind is a beautiful part of our body. It can easily take complete control over our thoughts. The mind is the wall of our heart.

Dark times are inescapable. Light and darkness live within each other and co-exist. You cannot have one without the other. This is the part we all share through understanding our own darkness. We cannot dispel the negative in our lives, but we can seek to find the positive within it.

I have created nine simple ways to overcome your difficulties:

• Go Where The Joy Is

It's important for us to go where the joy is when we are faced with unexpected news that could swallow us up, if we allow it. So, instead of letting the situation cloud your thinking, find the thing that brings you joy. Run to the source that brings you peace, comfort, and hope.

For me, it begins with God; next are my family and friends, and also things that bring me laughter and that I really enjoy doing! Refuse to stay stuck in that place and know that where you are or what you are dealing with is temporary and on its way to changing.

So ask yourself, "What brings me joy?" Then, make haste to go after that like never before!

Do Not Let Anyone Steal Your PEACE, JOY, And Happiness... It's Precious.

• Don't Engage In Risky Behaviours

People who are at the lowest moments of their life, coping with things like broken relationships, divorce, depression, or family loss, tend to give up on their life and, thinking it's so hard to carry on living, they often lose concern over their own well-being, thereby neglecting their personal hygiene and their physical appearance.

As a result, in most cases, they start engaging in risky behaviours, like drinking or drug use. Avoid alcohol, cigarettes and drugs. While these may make you feel good or numb your feelings for a while, the truth is that you will never live a fulfilled life. In fact, they will actually make your life even worse. Replace these things with your favourite hobbies, instead, to keep your body and mind relaxed.

• Be Honest With Yourself

We may think that, *if I just pretend it never happened, maybe it will all go away*. It sounds nice, but it's not true. Stop being in denial. Be honest about how you've messed up and be responsible and accept the consequences of your behaviour.

PERSPECTIVE

Is Often The Biggest Difference Between Struggle And Success.

YOU CAN CHANGE THE OUTCOME.

• Lose Yourself In Books And Find Yourself There

There is a reason for it. Not just that you learn when you read, but you get a new perspective when you read. A new way of looking at the same thing. I strongly believe that perspective is often the biggest difference between struggle and success.

If we can change perspective, we can change the story, and we can also change the outcome.
Books are a great way to change our perspective. If we study them and not just read them, it's like a journey through someone's mind.

Every time I read a new book, I would look for that one golden nugget that I could apply to my life to get the positive results I wanted, whatever it was. I would find that piece of wisdom and apply it to my life.

• Believe In Yourself And Never Limit Your Ability

If you are going to be successful in creating the life of your dreams, you have to believe that you are capable of making it happen. You have what it takes; the abilities, inner resources, talents and skills to create your desired results.

Have unwavering faith in yourself, for good and bad. Accepting this level of responsibility is uniquely empowering.

It means you can do, change, and be anything. Learning how to believe in yourself will effectively open up endless possibilities in your life. You must get rid of your fears and self-doubt in order to build self-esteem and self-confidence. Everything you have in your life is as a result of your self-belief.

Here are five important steps to apply. Practise them and you'll be amazed at the results:

1. Believe It And It Will Happen

Believe that you can always do it regardless of what anyone says or where you are in life.

2. Do Not Fear To Take First Steps

Many people fear to take risks in life. They are afraid of failure, afraid of criticism, fear poverty, afraid that they can't carry things through, or they are even waiting for all the circumstances to be just right before they start. Unfortunately, there are people that never undertake things that they would like to do in life just because they are afraid of not succeeding.

The thing is, if you want something badly enough, you don't sit and wait for it; instead, get together all the information you can find about it, all the equipment that is available and start what you can do at that time. On the way, chances are that things can be miraculously solved or placed at your service.

Persistence and

determination are key.

3. Visualise It

Think all the time about exactly what your life would look like if you had already achieved your dream.

One way to do this is with a motivational vision board. A vision board is a graphical representation of exactly what you want in life.

Print pictures from the Internet that represent what you want in life. Cut and stick them on your vision board. I have even put words that describe how I want to feel on a daily basis – such us "joyful", "abundant", "powerful", "healthy", "financial freedom", and "loved".

Take a few minutes to contemplate your vision board every day. Use it to visualise exactly where you want to go, and want to be or want to achieve.

4. Act As If It Has Already Happened

Always act in a way that is consistent with where you want to go and as if it has already happened. I recall one time when my bicycle was stolen from my property in Finsbury Park. I was very upset about it, I loved that bicycle so much and it was my favourite of all that I had ever used.

I was thinking of the bicycle all the time, looking for it everywhere, at the train station, throughout the neighbourhood, on the roads, etc. I told my husband that I would find it. One day, I was going home from Walthamstow College and for some reason I decided to take a different route that day, to take a train, which I had never done before.

As I was going into the station, I saw something that really took my attention. I turned my head quick again and guess what I saw? My bicycle! I waited for long hours from 11 a.m. to 5 p.m. to see if someone came to collect it, but no one turned up. I called the police and got my bicycle home!

5. Take Action

It is important to take action towards your goals. Do not let fear stop you. Nothing happens in life until you decide to take action.

Whatever you want is possible. I'll show you how to live your purpose and fulfil that empty feeling you may have been experiencing.

DREAM It, BELIEVE It, And DO It.

- ## Start Being Disciplined

I think, perhaps, disciplining yourself is one important thing that people need. This is a great subject that is given little attention. If you want to achieve your goal in life, then you have to discipline yourself. Plan what you want to achieve, keep your mind fixed on the things you want in life and off the things you don't want.

But the question is, how do you get disciplined?

How do you discipline yourself to achieve?

My method of exercising self-discipline consists of nine powerful steps. I have created these and associated with my inner ego that I need to be happy, successful, prosperous and healthful. You can use these to master self-discipline.

I would recommend these techniques to you, but if you prefer some other techniques your ideas may work just as well.

1. Turn Negative Thinking Into A Positive

Take possession of your own mind, and your thoughts. What our Creator intended every human being to do was to exercise complete control over his or her own mind, for their success and peace of mind. If you don't, you will become a victim, which then goes beyond your control.

Bad thoughts come to all of us and dominate our minds if we are not very careful. What do you do with these thoughts? Nowadays, we are bombarded with all kinds of things. *"It has been proven now scientifically that an affirmative thought is hundreds of times more powerful than a negative thought.'* – Michael Bernard Beckwith

The most important thing about negative feelings is that you have complete control over the way you think, the way you respond to any kind of situation and what you think about at any minute of the day. Filter what you see and hear. You can't turn off your hearing, but you can take out and cut off that chunk.

Accept responsibility for your life. Refuse to blame others or make excuses. You have the power to switch from one thought to another. It's you who can change the channel, because you have the remote control. Switch off. The problem is that people don't use the remote control – they leave it on the side. I had to exercise it, as I went along.

EVERYTHING BEGINS IN OUR THOUGHTS.

It's The Vehicle Of Our Destiny And To Our Success.

2. Know Your Weaknesses

Examine yourself very carefully. We all have weaknesses, whether that's snacking, fear, criticism, chocolate, and technology, just like Facebook or the latest addictive game application. Acknowledge your shortcomings, stumbling blocks or whatever they may be, then overcome them.

Too often people try to pretend nothing's wrong. You can't overcome shortcomings until you do acknowledge them, and take full control. Learn to improve yourself year after year.

3. Remove Temptation

Like the saying goes, "out of sight, out of mind". It may seem silly, but this phrase offers powerful advice. By simply removing your biggest temptations from your environment, you will greatly improve your self-discipline. We gain strength over temptation when we resist.

If you want to eat healthier, toss the junk food in the bin. If you want to improve your productivity at work, turn off social media notifications and silence your cell phone. You can be more focused on accomplishing your goals. Set yourself up for success by ditching bad influences. We gain the strength of temptation when we resist.

4. Set Goals And Remove Limitations

If you want to achieve self-discipline, you must have a clear vision of what you want to accomplish in life, and also to understand what success means to you. If you don't know where you are going, it's easy to lose your way. A clear plan outlines each step you must take in order to reach your goals.

Remove limitations, and aim for something bigger. In a great country like this, with abundant opportunity, there is no reason for anybody limiting himself or herself – aim for something greater and take possession.

Your Vision Will Become Clear Only When You LOOK INTO YOUR OWN HEART.

5. Take Simple Steps

We aren't born with self-discipline – it's a learned behaviour. And, just like any other skill you want to master, it requires daily practise and repetition. Don't try to change everything at once, focus on doing one thing at a time, consistently, with that goal in mind.

For example, if you're trying to get in shape, start by working out for ten or fifteen minutes a day. If you're trying to achieve better sleep habits, start by going to bed fifteen minutes earlier each night. Take baby steps. Eventually, when you're ready, you can add more goals to your list.

6. Use Your Time Wisely

I want to emphasise the necessity for self-discipline in connection with one particular subject and that is the use of time. Time is a very important factor. I was very guilty of not appreciating that. We must use self-discipline to control our use of time. Time is the greater healer of our adversities and struggles.

We are often over-cluttered with information. Everywhere we go we have information that is distracting us from the things we need to do, and the things that we want to do. Since the time we have is our most valuable resource, we need to learn how to use it in the best possible way.

To do that, you need to answer two questions:
1. What do I want to achieve in life?
2. How do I need to use my time to accomplish that?

Isn't it interesting that every single person in the world has the same exact amount of time in a day? How interesting that every person who lives on Earth is given a gift consisting of exactly 1,440 minutes every single day. Don't give them away easily. No one who lives is given more or given less.

We are free to spend those minutes how we choose, but we can't save them, and every minute that is wasted is gone forever. As Benjamin Franklin said: "Lost time is never found again." We can use our time to improve ourselves and help others or we can waste our time on Earth pursuing activities that are not meaningful or are even harmful.

The choice is ours to make.

One of the easiest ways to become better at this is to take one day at a time. So, make sure to control how you spend your time wisely. Otherwise, you will end up three hours later on YouTube watching a random cat video that offers no significant benefit to your life.

7. Correct Past Failures, Be Patient, Learn And Adapt

I had to use my past failures and learn to have patience for things to happen in their own time. You've got to have a lot of patience to stay on the right track. Most of us know that failure is a reality of life, and at some level, we understand that it actually helps us to grow.

But still, we hate to fail, we fear it, we dread it. Failure doesn't define your identity. Just because you haven't yet found a successful way of doing something doesn't mean *you are a failure.* You keep trying until you find the way. Be patient.

You know that you have to sow the seeds before your reap the fruit of your work, but the majority of people in the world are trying to reap without sowing. Everything in life you get that's worthy has a price tagged into it and it's not cheap and doesn't come easily. It requires lots of patience and hard work.

8. Change Your Perception About Willpower

Most of our bad habits are due to laziness or lack of willpower. If you believe you have a limited amount of willpower, you probably won't surpass those limits. If you don't place a limit on your self-control, you are less likely to exhaust yourself before meeting your goals.

9. Control The Power Of Your Emotions

Some of the other major enemies to positive human emotions are hatred and anger and jealousy and fear and revenge and greed and egoism and vanity and the desire for something and nothing. You'll never make any accurate decision in order to think or deal with facts when you're angry – remember that.

As long as you allow these emotions, the positive or the negative, to take possession of you, you will never be able to do logical thinking. I don't mean that you can shut off your emotions entirely, but I do say that you can use self-discipline to keep all these emotions under control at all times, instead of letting those emotions rule you.

Let your head do the thinking, not your heart.

Chapter 3
My Golden Rules For Breakthrough To Success

Some Great Tips To Make Your Goals Your Reality

There are certain common features that successful people exhibit and that anyone can practice. They are what can jumpstart your success and attract what you want in life. You'd be hard pressed to find any high achiever who doesn't live by the following twelve tips:

1. Be Grateful

How many people start their day with gratitude even before touching their phone or getting out of bed? If you create a daily habit, just for a few minutes, to express gratitude for everything you progressed in and achieved so far, you will gain huge confidence. This is powerful, because you can't be grateful and feel negative emotions at the same time.

After you do this, you will see two things that will happen:

1. You will start to see progress with your goals.

2. You will want to set and achieve more goals because it feels great.

BE GRATEFUL

Every Day, Even For Little Things. You Can't Be Trusted With Bigger Things If You Don't Appreciate Small Things.

2. Get Passionate

When you are true to yourself and passionate about what you do, you choose to see choice rather than the challenge that sits right in your face. Your true essence is not set up on false pretences because whatever paths you choose in life, personal and professional, are completely congruent with who you are.

One of the most powerful qualities you can possess is a genuine passion for your goal. Passion is vital because fervent desire for your goal will fire you on and press you towards it even quicker. This is key to success.

3. Set Goals And Be Focused

Known as the Pareto Principle, in most cases, 80 percent of results come from only 20 percent of activities. Ultra-productive people know which activities drive the greatest results. Focus on those and ignore the rest. If you have your goals and stay focused specifically on what you want, you will be able to have a clear picture of what you want to achieve.

But, if it is out of focus and you have no goals, then your picture will be blurry. All you need to do is to set the goals that will indeed make the difference in your life and go one day at a time.

4. Create A Map Towards Your Goal

The act of making a map and a plan showing how you will get to your goals forces the brain to think about it. As we think about it, we find ideas, strategies that otherwise would stay hidden in our subconscious. Goals with plans and follow-through are a powerful fuel for success.

Do not concentrate on the problem, but rather, concentrate on what you can do to get out of that messy situation. Be positive, be determined, be focused, and never give up. Work, research, and improve until you give birth to that dream. Never let go, because if you don't grab it, someone else will gobble it up.

5. Stop Multitasking!

It might seem productive to multitask, and in some ways it can be, but it has been scientifically proven that multitasking weakens your mental aptitude. Your brain's ability to get back to work on one task after you've interrupted it wastes time and money. Stop doing it.

Direct your concentration towards one thing at a time and do that to the best of your ability, put in 100 percent of your effort.

6. Write Things Down

Richard Branson has said on more than one occasion that he wouldn't have been able to build Virgin without a simple notebook, which he takes with him wherever he goes. He knew the value of writing things down. Write things down on paper, so that you will have a snapshot of where you stand and where you want to be.

It will boost your productivity. Writing things down enables a higher level of thinking, and therefore, more focused action. Include your situation, food situation, finances, and how you will solve them. Make your goals real by recording them. Make them the centre of your focus. Don't just set them and then ignore them.

Greek tycoon Aristotle Onassis said, "Always carry a notebook. Write everything down … That is a million dollar lesson they don't teach you in business school!"

How to set and accomplish goals:
- Commit – write it down as a form of commitment.
- State your "why" – why it's important to you, and what benefits you will get.
- Set a deadline – keep your deadlines reasonable to avoid procrastination.
- Set rewards – to motivate you more.
- Plan ahead – identify obstacles you might face, come up with solutions to overcome them and eliminate excuses.

If you start with a blank piece of paper, then it will be easier to have a fresh start. These are the easiest to attain again. Then, on another new sheet of paper, write out your forgotten resources. These are your most valuable, and oftentimes difficult to realise again.

Also write down the things you know you're good at. Things like:

- How to speak and write English.
- How to manage time effectively.
- How to use a computer.
- How to access the Internet.
- How to listen.

I am sure you will need many sheets of paper to keep writing down what you know. Afterwards, concentrate on the things that you can achieve, exactly as you have achieved others.

7. Make One Business Connection

You've probably heard the expression, "It's not what you know. It's *who* you know." Well, this is true for every area of life, but it's especially true when it comes to your career.

There are many ways to improve your business. But here are six resources that you can use to get started:

1. <u>LinkedIn</u>: The best social media site for making business connections and profiling your skills, knowledge, and areas of expertise.

2. <u>Beyond</u>: Another social media site for professionals, with over fifty million registered members.

3. <u>Meetup</u>: The preferred site for finding specific groups in the area and connecting with people who are interested in your career field.

4. <u>Facebook Groups</u>: One of the best resources for finding people who share a mutual interest. There are millions of groups here, so it's not hard to find a few that specialise in your industry.

5. <u>Fiverr:</u> Is an online marketplace for freelance services, and provides a platform for freelancers to offer services to customers worldwide.

6. Use the Coach.me App: The <u>Coach.me</u> app is a free app and a great tool for maintaining and sticking to new habits. It's more like having a coach in your pocket. You'll be held accountable for your activities and goals. Meet other members who celebrate their goal achievement at the end of the day.

This app will help you to:

● Visualise your progress.

● Receive step-by-step coaching (on specific habits or goals).

● Develop winning habits.

● Get encouragement from friends and strangers.

8. Seek Continuous Education

Lifelong learning is extremely practical these days and does not require as much effort as it did in the past. In these days of advanced technology and the Internet, anything you can imagine is at your fingertips ... You can watch YouTube videos to learn new skills, and also take online courses to earn a degree.

When you're constantly pushing yourself to learn new things, your mental health also improves. Research shows that an active and engaged mind improves overall cognitive ability. The more you educate yourself, the more humble you become. That is already proven.

You'll improve your self-worth as it teaches you to step outside of your comfort zone, which will undoubtedly improve your confidence. *You'll also connect better with others* by expanding your knowledge base. Learning exposes you to a multitude of new ideas and perspectives that you may have otherwise never considered before.

9. Take A Small Step In The Right Direction

Sometimes, the smallest step in the right direction ends up being the biggest step to achieve your dream life. After the accident, I suffered not only physically and emotionally, but we suffered huge financial loss as well. I knew that there were a myriad of opportunities out there that I needed to access in order to go to the top to accomplish my goals.

After attending many courses and programmes, I signed up to the Speakers are Leaders programme. I was happy with what this programme offered to me, as it was exactly what I had been searching for. After two years of picking up the phone, calling mentors, attending events, buying services, long hours of training, etc., I could see the light at the end of the tunnel.

I believe that I will have an audience who will be willing to buy products from me. So, I pulled out my notebook and started to write out the script for my first book, *Born To*

Stand Out, Not To Fit In: Empower Yourself To Live An Extraordinary Life. I took the simplest step that I could.

I built a prototype product over the duration of the course, and then offered that product to my list. Now, I was on to something. Wherever you are right now in your life, do not focus on the gap. There's a giant space between you and where you want to be.

Just take the next bold step and, before you know it, your life will look completely different from where you started.

10. Plan Actions From Your Goals

Goals are not just items for your to-do list. Your goal is what you are striving for. Specifically plan actions that lead you towards those goals. Use your goals to provide your compass for those actions. When you plan actions for the day, you can easily tell if they're going to be effective if only you have clear goals to compare them against.

11. Don't Give Up

Don't be afraid to try something, fail and try something else. Take effective and massive action to meet your goals, and understand that any true goal will take many steps to be achieved. Sometimes you will make a misstep, but that doesn't mean that there's something wrong with the goal.

Everyone makes mistakes, but it's only those who abandon their goals that don't achieve them. Don't be one of them!

Chapter 4
Unbreakable, Unshakable, Unsinkable Soul

Raise Above The Impossible

Often, we see other people's struggles and hardships as they go through life, but we never think that it could happen to us. "The challenge she's facing isn't my challenge. It's not going to happen to me, I'm young and I'm healthy, I will not face what she's facing." That's how my perception was.

I was thinking that having a baby when I was "ready" would be easy. I was wrong! I was ready, waiting, and practically dying to be pregnant, waiting and hoping that next month will be my dream month. I can't imagine how many disappointing mornings I had when I woke up to discover, yet again, that my period came – in despair, I would cry and complain.

Months, years, of charting my ovulation without results and then testing on dozens of ovulation sticks with ambiguous results. I didn't care about anything anymore, I just wanted a baby! I Googled all possible ways to become pregnant. All the time, I would think about becoming pregnant, my life was hijacked, focusing on having a baby.

I would have daydreams and night dreams. It was so heartbreaking. I was hurt deeply, felt incomplete, and rejected. I was looking at mums' bumps, mums holding their babies, mums that were pushing prams, women who had just given birth and the euphoria they felt, and I compared them to me.

It felt like I was getting punched right into my heart. I was extremely jealous of other pregnant women. It was pregnancy that I was desperate for, not someone else's baby. I felt grief that I might never experience this wonderful experience. I considered them very blessed.

It was so hard for me to stay happy. I just pretended to be happy. I had a disguised smile, disguised beauty, looking beautiful just on the outside. I had always been a positive thinker and a believer, and I forced myself to once again start thinking positive and regain all the hope.

One of the hardest moments would be when someone announced she was pregnant, or a friend was pregnant. They were not happy tears; they were ugly, dark tears of incredulous jealousy. *She only got married a few months earlier, and is pregnant. I am the one who is supposed to be pregnant! What is happening to me? What sort of life is this without children?*

They would proceed delicately, afraid of opening my tearful floodgates, and I didn't want to talk about it. One Monday morning, I was having breakfast with my husband. He left for work and I was still sitting drinking my tea. I wasn't happy, I was like a dead body, just breathing, completely empty. That void inside of me, just thinking of a BABY!

Suddenly a thought popped into my mind. PRAY. I remember that vividly. I went to my bedroom and started to pray. I was very angry, revolted, disgusted. I wrestled with God, I blamed Him for my life. I blamed Him for all my unhappiness and suffering. I questioned Him about why my life was this way.

"God, here I am, miserable, childless, and unhappy. Why? Do you really love me? How can a Father let His daughter suffer? Do you really exist? I always have loved You, my situation does not glorify You. Be attentive and listen to my prayer.

By next year, if I don't have a child, I will never believe in You again – never! I will never believe that You really exist." I gave God a deadline – that's right ... a deadline. I did just that. "This is my test to You," I said. "You prove Your existence." I said exactly this.

"I know You love me, but how come the birds in the air and the dogs on the ground have a family and I don't? Why not me? Am I not worth much more than the birds and the dogs?" Hot tears were shooting from my eyes, my shirt was completely wet.

I finished my powerful prayer and emptied everything into God's hands. I wiped my face, got up and said, "I will never nag or ask You again for the same thing. I have done my part. Now it's Your turn. I leave it in Your hands." As soon as I finished my prayer I felt a complete sense of relief.

I felt different. A heavy burden was taken from my shoulders. I felt incredible peace, joy, as if God Himself had audibly spoken to me: "It's going to be fine, you will have a child." I knew in that very moment that my prayer had reached heaven. I had received the answer that I was waiting desperately for, for so long.

After a couple of months of saying that prayer I was feeling different. I understood that my body wasn't acting right. I just knew it, I had the insurance inside me. Even the world could come against me, none could change my belief that I was pregnant. I took a pregnancy test. I was pregnant!

I treasured that moment, beyond all human comprehension, that amazing feeling, the challenge of waiting and testing my strength never took my faith way. I am proud of myself and I am sure God is, too.

I loved being pregnant.

I loved my belly – that feeling of the baby acknowledging the miracle, that was capable of producing a whole other being from scratch, inside of me.

I cried … this time, tears of JOY.

She's born! We welcomed our daughter, Helena, in January 2009.

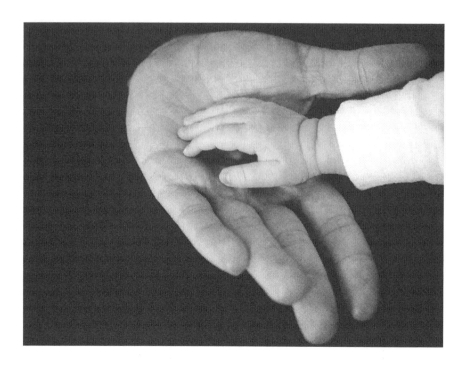

The first time I heard her cry as she was surgically removed from my belly, I felt truly blessed. He fulfilled His promise by reminding me: "Here's your sweet baby daughter, take care of her, it's your responsibility to bring her up in God's instruction."

What an awesome task. God even blessed us with a son, three years later. I felt like a woman for the first time, I had an all-round sensation of power. My kids are my priority, the light of my everyday life, my sunshine, those smiles, those eyes, my audience. What an amazing joy!

My daughter, my firstborn, an answer to many prayers! She's not part of my body anymore, she has her own fingerprints, her own DNA, and her own blood type, perfectly made.

After thirteen years of waiting, the "Impossible" became "Possible". It feels truly like heaven sent on Earth!

Chapter 5
Leveraging The Power Of Spirituality To Attain Success

We are already spiritual. We are divinely connected to each other and to the universe as a whole. Never underestimate the strength of your soul by living in an authentic way that sets you on your own unique path. *You don't have a soul, you are a soul – it lights within you.*

Stand strong in your uniqueness and your vital energy print. We seek perfection, yet it is something we already have – it lies in being perfectly free to just be who we are. We all are on a journey of self-discovery and self-knowledge to become wiser, more enlightened and strengthened from a place deep inside.

It is only when we begin to uncover the truth of our inner strength and awaken our inner fire that we can realise our power for change, transformation, success, happiness release from shackles, or other physical restraints.

As You Eat Food For Your Physical Body, TAKE CARE OF YOUR SPIRITUAL LIFE.

Spiritual Personal Development

The importance of the spiritual life, mental activity, and physical exercise are all equally important and must be in balance to allow the symphony of your life to play harmoniously. Your own inner genius is not all about IQ and inventing the world's next big thing. *It's about never losing sight of the big thing that is alive in you,* moving through you and for you alone.

You will learn how to super-charge your soul and naturally boost your self-esteem, maintain motivation and keep your spiritual light burning very bright. You are more powerful than you've ever believed yourself to be and this book shows you that you've been in possession of the keys all along.

All of those can create different paths for you to experience, but at the centre of every experience *you will always find yourself.* In this chapter, you will learn simple, yet dynamic, methods found at the heart of every spiritual path. Find out how divine transformation is always ready for you, and patiently waiting for your discovery.

You will explore what you stand for, how to talk with your spiritual source, how to overcome everything, and how to live out your most successful divine life.

SPIRITUALITY
Is Good For
Your Soul,
And You Will Find
It To Be Very
Empowering.

Spirituality Does Not Come From Religion, It Comes From Your Soul

Spirituality is not a religion, as many people think it to be. Being mystical means that you are in touch with your own divine, the source itself. Being Spiritually Strong means becoming powerful because of Spiritual Knowledge, Spiritual intelligence, Spiritual Understanding, which gives us the strength to face situations, people, etc., which you can't just face with your physical strength or mental strength.

Hence, rather than complaining always to others, you should evaluate within and ask yourself what you are doing about yourself, about your anger, attachment, pride, and jealousy.

These are some things that you have to check regularly in your day-to-day life.

3 Good Reasons Why Being More Spiritual Is Important:

1. You become aware of your environment and in full control of your own life.

2. You become better focused than you've ever been, you will enhance your energy level, and your effectiveness will increase.

3. You'll become happier, more confident, and more accomplished in life. What I have learned from my experiences will help you to be empowered spiritually, mentally, emotionally, and physically. Take imperfect action – move in the right direction, even if it's not up to 100 percent.

9 Transformational Steps Towards
Spiritual Self-Mastery

1. Be Personally Accountable

When you're personally accountable, you stop assigning blame to anyone else. You stop putting "if's" on people, and making excuses. On the long and winding road of life, choose accountability at every turn.

According to Professor Emeritus Marcia Rachel of the University of Mississippi Medical Center – who has written about accountability – there are different definitions of accountability.

All of them involve five key ideas:

Obligation – a responsibility to accomplish a task.

Willingness – taking actions because you want to, rather than because you have to.

Intent - the reason behind every action.

Ownership – taking responsibility for your behaviour and outcomes.

Commitment – dedicating yourself to the task or goal at hand.

2. Extend Grace To Others And Ask The Spirit For Grace For Yourself

Learn to forgive others, as God forgave you. When we talk about God's grace we think straight to the point of Him giving us His Son for our salvation. My favourite definition of God's grace is: God giving us what we don't deserve in any way. We deserve nothing, yet by His mercy and grace we are saved.

Showing grace to others is a matter of dealing kindly with them, even if we are sure that they don't deserve it.

7 Great Ways To Show Grace

1. Respond With A Smile

A quick response with anger will leave you seething. But the sooner you can respond with a smile and a calm spirit, the sooner you will be able to see the truth embedded in their words and make the changes that need to be made.

2. Use Words Showing Grace

When speaking with people, you should use words that are kind and gentle. Obviously, there are times when we need to correct other people, but it never has to be done in a hateful or mean-spirited way. Find a way to gently say what needs to be said.

3. Forgive With Grace

When someone asks for forgiveness, accept their apology graciously. They have come to you humbly asking for your pardon. That is not a time to tell them why, just separate your advice from your forgiveness. Allow them to see that you have accepted their apology, and then later share with them the correction and direction that they need to walk with.

4. Say "I'm Sorry"

Remember, grace is giving to the other person what in actual fact they don't deserve. When you make a mistake, swallow your pride and ask for forgiveness. Maybe they wronged you in some way, but you responded inappropriately. What's the point?

You can ask them to forgive you for your response. Even if, in your opinion, they don't deserve an apology, you can ask their forgiveness for your wrong response.

5. Forgive Quickly

When you need to apologise, do it quickly. Forgive, even if they don't ask for it. Grace can go a long way in repairing a relationship if you respond in a loving way, even when they don't.

6. Clean Up Your Language

Be careful how you express yourself. Do you have some words in your vocabulary that shouldn't be there? There may be some words you say that aren't really "bad" words, but the way you say them expresses the same feelings and emotions as others who use the real bad words.

7. Say "Thank You" To Show Grace

Say "thank you." It doesn't cost you anything, it's "free", but it can show other people gratitude and grace. Write a simple card expressing your appreciation for an act of kindness on your behalf. You can make a difference by putting a "thank you" on your lips or a card in someone's hand.

3. You Can Heal Yourself!

If we are willing to do the mental work, almost anything can be healed. I have a great deal of experience and first-hand information to share about healing, including how I overcome it for myself. What we think about ourselves becomes the truth for us.

I believe that everyone, including me, is responsible for everything that happens in our lives, for the best and the worst.

4. Cultivate Your Power And Don't Allow Anyone To Take It From You!

We feel sadness, guilt or anger because of OTHER people. As hard as it seems, we need to learn how to identify the moment when we give our power away and how we can retain it. It is easier said than done, and it is something that everyone has to continuously work on. But, identifying how we give our power away is the first step!

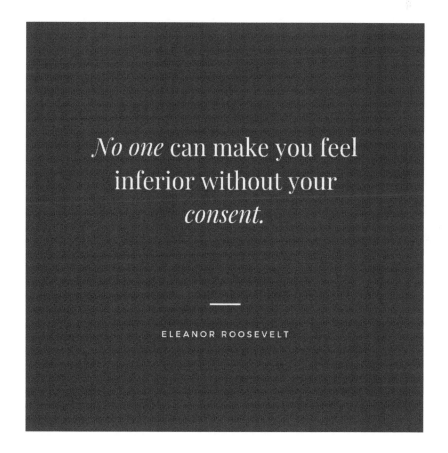

> *No one* can make you feel inferior without your *consent.*
>
> ELEANOR ROOSEVELT

Here are Three Proven Lessons How:

1. Take Control Of Your Life

No matter what happens in life, you have a choice. If you are in a job you do not like, go in search of a new one. If you do not like how you look, then take good care of your body, your health, your eating habits. In life, there are things that you should do and there are always consequences, both for actions taken and the ones not taken. However, you always have a choice.

2. Let Go Of Grudges

Are you still angry over something that happened five years ago? Let it go! Holding a grudge in your heart will not make the situation any better, and it most certainly will not change what happened. Staying mad only leads to more stress, and it makes you less powerful in the eyes of whoever you are angry with.

3. Don't Change Your Goals Because Of Negative Feedback

No one became successful overnight and we should never expect it to be different for us. If you are passionate about a project and want to achieve a goal, do not give up because of one moment of failure. And do not give up because someone said they did not believe in you or in your goal.

If you do this, you are allowing failure and other people define who you are! Have confidence in yourself and your dreams and "Just Do It!"

5. Develop Spiritual Gifts Through Practicing Prophecy, Healing And Manifestation

God has created every person to be a supernatural spiritual, with the capacity to function not only in a natural world, but also to have access to the realm of the spirit, access where God is, and to bring Heaven to Earth.

God's desire is that you should be a channel for Heaven coming to Earth, for His presence, goodness, healing, love, peace and prosperity to flow through you, and to manifest in the world around you. His plan is that the kingdom will come into the earth through you.

All you've got to do is learn how to do it.

6. Dream Big ...

Don't let your inner devil's advocate inhibit you from dreaming big. As soon as you commit to a big dream, go after it, your subconscious creative mind will come up with big ideas to make it happen. Learn how to think big, take your dreams and turn them into big business reality.

Every day is filled with new opportunities, fresh perspectives and business goals. You'll soon start attracting the people, resources, and opportunities you need to make your dream come true. Big dreams not only inspire you, but they also compel others to want to play big, too. Map your dreams to reality.

Winning in business starts with a winning mindset. Let's get started on learning to think big by following these three simple steps:

Tip 1: Start With A Dream

A dream is defined as a hope or wish for something in the future, such as a desired situation or goal. Every great leader was, in fact, a great dreamer. No successful company ever started without a dream, hope or wish for the future. Dreams are the fundamental building blocks of great success.

"All men dream, but not equally. Those who dream by night in the dusty recesses of their minds, wake in the day to find that it was vanity: but the dreamers of the day are

dangerous men, for they may act on their dreams with open eyes, to make them possible." T.E. Lawrence

Tip 2: The Creative Imagination Dream

A dream coupled with imagination is quite powerful. Imagination is the simplest form of the mind that helps create the process of creation, which is a powerful tool. Moving from a dream to creation is the next important step. Start imagining what "could be" and approach your goals with solution-based scenarios.

Tip 3: The Spark Of ... An Idea

An idea is defined as something, such as a thought or concept, that potentially or actually exists in the mind as a product of mental activity – they don't actually exist, yet many people are waiting for that great idea – the thing that will take them from the life that they are living to the life they actually want to be living.

Once you make a decision to start dreaming and tap into your imagination, ideas will soon follow.

7. Surround Yourself With Supportive And Like-Minded People

Why should you surround yourself with like-minded people? Whenever I am at conferences or meetings, I learn a lot, but the thing that stands out the most is the importance of surrounding yourself with like-minded people, because you feel a sense of belonging, not judgement, for who you truly are.

When you surround yourself with like-minded people, it can help you:

- Stay Motivated
- Grow
- Make Positive Decisions
- Know Yourself
- Ask Questions
- Spark Ideas
- Be Yourself

These meetings motivate me in many more ways than one. I feel so inspired to mingle with like-minded people, with a positive mindset. I want to grow further in many aspects of my life. I also made a lot of positive decisions. I learned never to be afraid to ask questions, they may spark new ideas.

Lastly, I loved that I could truly be myself around these people.

NO GOD,
NO HOPE,
NO DIRECTION,
NO WAY OUT.

Without Him,
We Are Like Fish
Without Water.

8. Don't Be Discouraged!

Living by faith in things not seen is hard. The word of God reminds us: We cannot please God without faith. Many have suffered far more and have remained faithful ... don't give up when your long asked-and-sought prayers have not yet been answered.

"God will give you His grace in your time of need, and it will be sufficient for you, even in the very worst times."

9. Pay Attention To Signs From The Spirit

One thing that I am sure of is, I have evaluated. I covered the whole process in lots of prayer and the leading soon became clear. What started as questioning became an unwavering certainty that God was, in fact, redirecting me to His path.

Reroute
Your Way
In God's Way

What Does God's Direction Look Like?

1. Passions Shift

I still wholeheartedly believe that our plans are not God's plan. Becoming a teacher is a wonderful job, which I always deeply cherished in my heart. But, as God fanned the flames of my passion for positive parenting, empowering, writing, and public speaking, He allowed my passion for children to dwindle in a different way of helping.

2. Confirmation Of Godly Counsel

Proverbs 11:14 tells us: "Where there is no guidance, a people falls, but in an abundance of counsellors there is safety." As I shared this experience with close friends, they were able to pose questions I hadn't considered, and to ultimately confirm their agreement that my decision was sound.

3. Sound Decision

While these clues led me to believe the fact that I had made a solid choice, making a change like this still required me to step out in faith. God didn't write an answer in the sky or on my forehead. I strongly believe that God has been leading me through each step, to meeting with the right people, making the right connections, changing my heart, providing opportunities, closing doors that needed to be closed in my life. We have such a faithful Father to lead us so gently!

Before the decision was final, there came a time when I claimed the truth of Proverbs 3:5-6, and prayed something like this:

"Father, you know that I just want to honour You with this decision. I want to glorify Your name. It's not about me anymore, it's about helping others. What You have given me, much is required from me. Let Your Will be accomplished in this matter. I believe this is the direction in which You're leading me, but if I am wrong, I trust You to prevent me from continuing on this path. If it's not from You and it is for my destruction, take it away from my heart. Please lead me as You've promised to do when I acknowledge You."

I believe God has been prodding and encouraging me to keep praying for His understanding and wisdom.

I have been fighting this thought and asking this question at the back of my mind. What is my public figure and my Bible character? One day, I was meditating on these thoughts that pretty much answered my prayers. "Walk with me ..." With my eyes closed, I saw something in a vision, writing "EYES" in beautiful colourful letters.

Thoughts were flowing through my heart and my mind.

For some time, I didn't understand what God was trying to say to me with this word. Later on, things started to make sense and become much clearer.

WALK WITH GOD,

Let Him LEAD, FOLLOW Him.

His Plans For Us Are For Good, And Not Evil.

Don't Compromise Your Faith

We live in a fallen world where people are so much convinced that they are the master of their own fate. Yet, God has another plan that He declares is to prosper us. Too often, we believe it is okay to compromise our faith, belief system, and moral values for the sake of getting what we think we deserve in life.

We should never compromise our faith for the sake of man or worldly possessions. Nor should we let anything prevent us from believing that God is our source of provision and is in total control of all our affairs. I was convinced beyond doubt that this was just a test of my faith.

And I never questioned God, asking "Why?" While the circumstance may be painful, I always looked at it as a form of blessing. Leave the rest to Him. We mustn't do what evildoers do. Faith in God does not make our troubles disappear, it only makes trouble appear less frightening, because it puts them in the right perspective.

We are subject to the same actions and laws. Don't settle for something less than what you believe in. Do not compromise your faith for the sake of others or what you think you deserve. This, for some, can be easier said than done. And for others with faith, it can easily be done.

We may not want to experience discomfort and pain, but it may be best for us because God may be working through us, and preparing us for something greater. He uses that experience so that we become better and not bitter.

Suffering Promotes
CHARACTER
And Provokes
COURAGE.

Faith And Spiritual Practice

Most importantly, maintain faith that things will get better because they always do, in the long run, as long as you keep the momentum going. When you are at rock bottom, it's easy to believe that there's no hope around. What does not kill you can only make you stronger, if you step into the light.

Find the fire within you. Keep in mind that you are one thought and one step away from the light. This can help to build courage, gratitude, and hope for the future. Your priorities should be:

1.   Leave things behind and project your sense-of-self forward.

2. Find balance in life spiritually, mentally, emotionally, and physically.

Eventually, you will feel like life is in a state of momentum. You will feel more productive, but not in a stressful way.

You May Be Materially Blessed, But You Can Be Spiritually

CORRUPTED

Chapter 6
Learn How To Find Your Passion And Life Purpose

What Is Your Purpose?

Have you ever thought about this question? Do you feel like you are fulfilling your purpose through your job roles? All you have to do is to ensure that what you're chasing is meaningful to you; this will bring focus and motivation as you strive to achieve your goals.

If you have your purpose defined, then that's amazing! You know what drives you and why. But if you don't feel like you have a purpose nailed down, it's good to start by asking, "*why ...?*" For example, *why* are you working in your particular job or industry?

If the reason is vague or unclear, you may find yourself not having a direction for where you're headed in life.

Stop Moaning, Complaining And Having Self-Pity.

Get Up And Do Something About It.

How To Find Your Passion And Purpose In Life

If you want to be fulfilled, content, and experience inner peace, it's very important that you learn how to find your passion and life purpose. Without a life purpose your goals and action plans may not ultimately fulfil you. When you master habits and motivation, you will start seeing big results.

1. Explore The Things You Love To Do And What Comes Easy To You

We are all born with a deep and meaningful purpose that we have to discover. Your purpose is not something you need to make up, it's already in there. You have to uncover it in order to create the life you want. You may ask yourself, "What is my purpose in life?" You can begin to discover your passion or your purpose by exploring two things.

Alternatively, you may enjoy what you do, but on deeper exploration discover that you're passionate about something altogether different than what you do.

Consider that your calling is simply an outflow of two things: loving God and loving people. Tackle daily challenges, live with passion and purpose, and realise all your ambitions. Ask yourself if you're adding to it is something that feeds your ego or pride, or simply makes you believe that you'll ultimately have some sort of fulfilment through that career that really, only God can supply, and no one can lead you to this path other than God Himself.

Usually, we're called to do the hard thing. The unselfish thing. The sacrificial thing. Yes, He uses people in our lives and circumstances, but He really is the only one who can give us peace and certainty about what He has for us. No one should tell you what your calling in life is.

Turn off the voices that are so sure they know what you should be doing with your life. Listen to the voices that point you back to God. I am doing what I AM called to do, and not what I feel or what others think. Finding my purpose in life is the most fundamental part of my life, and I advise you to invest so as to find what's yours.

I am on the right track, heading in the right direction. I know where I am heading to. I am aligning my personality with my purpose that I am being called to do. Why I am here! and I am happy that I have found my true identity.
Keep this in mind − I do this because is my calling. Not my job, not my work, not my gig − my calling!

LIVE BY CHOICE.

Not By Chance.

MAKE

CHANGES

Not Excuses.

Encourage Yourself And Others

I have always been an encouraging person and a good motivator for my kids, my loved ones, and my friends. When they need help or advice concerning their life struggles, they ask me for advice. So, I believe that my being has a positive influence in their life.

Those around you become energised by your positivity, personality, honesty and your encouragement to progress in their personal life, going forward.

What Message Am I Sending To People With My Actions?

Aim to live a life that is beyond success – one full of purpose, joy, and personal fulfilment. There is nothing of greater significance than to offer your life with your good action and helping others out in what you know so well.
Ralph Waldo Emerson said: "Your actions speak so loudly, I can not hear what you are saying."

Send messages of self-empowerment, live an extraordinary life, practice positive parenting, live with authority, love, kindness, empathy and trust. Be truthful. Understand why being truthful is very important, including to yourself. The one thing you cannot afford to lose is your honesty.

Once that is lost due to dishonesty, it may be impossible to recover. Living from the truth allows you to build relationships based on trust between you and your loved ones, colleagues, competitors, staff and customers.

Be Prepared To Meet The Opportunity

I am grateful and thankful for everything I have and all that has happened to me. Surely, without it, I would not be the person that I am today. That was a preparation for me to meet the opportunity. You have to be grateful for your family or friends that value your voice and listen to you; you create value and add value into their life, and lift your spirit and their spirit high.

I am grateful for everything in my life when I get up in the morning. I open the window and see the beauty around me. How can you doubt the infinity of the creation of the universe? I explain this with the watchmaker analogy. In the same way as you see a watch, you would identify there is a designer.

When you look at the beauty of nature and, most specifically, the complexity of us human beings, you can assume there is a designer, because it's like the watch.

WORK ON FINDING YOUR IDENTITY

And Pursue Them In Life.

Tapping Into Your Identity

In order to get to where you want to be, here are some questions for you to answer:

- Find your talents. What are you good at?
- Find your passions. What do you love to do? Help others with that passion.
- What's your identity? Who are you? Why are you here on Earth?
- What opportunities are out there for you to take or create?

Play around, experiment, and you will be able to find yours. But understand that this is a never-ending process. It's not just about you, anymore, it's about helping other souls. Everyone might not take my message, but if I reach even a single one who shares the same value and the same belief, and I know that I helped that soul, it will make my day.

PURSUE YOUR OPPORTUNITIES And Consider Yourself Blessed.

Humble Yourself

Lust, envy, anger, greed are all bad, but pride is the deadliest of all – it is the root of all evil. Proud people are too arrogant. It's incredibly frustrating when dealing with someone who simply refuses to admit their weakness or accept criticism. If you want to receive God's grace in a unique way, seek to consistently humble yourself.

We shouldn't need any more reasons than this. I don't know about you, but I don't want God resisting me and I need all the grace I can get. I also want to receive as much grace as possible. How do I receive grace? By just humbling myself before God.

Humbling yourself and accepting what you need to change is the beginning of your character transformation. The sad thing is that people who really are in need of help refuse to admit it. They are too proud to ask for help from those around them.

Many relationship issues are caused by pride. If you can't admit that you're wrong, it's your pride telling you to "win" the argument. A proud man is always looking down on things and as long as you are focused on looking down, you cannot see something that is above you.

GOD'S GRACE

Is Like An Ocean That Overwhelms Us With Love.

Do You Know The Three Most Dangerous Words In Your Vocabulary?

The three most dangerous words in the human vocabulary that hold people back from success are: "I know that."

If you think that you know everything, then you close yourself off from learning. My belief is that you don't actually know something until you are doing it.

You need to live it in your life and in your business, because if you aren't implementing what you know, you don't really know it. The most successful people in the world are always trying to learn and improve; also, they are the most humble ones, because they understand that there is always more they could do.

They understand that there is value in everything. Knowledge and virtue are inseparable. Right thinking and right doing can never be separated.

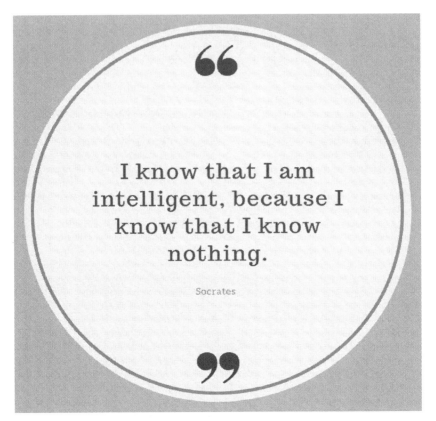

I know that I am intelligent, because I know that I know nothing.

Socrates

When you achieve success, it is important that you don't let it go to your head. Humility is a vital component for achieving success in all areas of life. Stay confident, put arrogance aside as you strive to achieve your goals, and draw a fine line between confidence and arrogance.

The confident person will say, "I can do it," whereas the arrogant person will say, "only I can do it."

Chapter 7
How To Create A Healthy Body And Mind To Be Happy And Balanced Every Day

1. Stop Feeling Overwhelmed And Start Progressing Towards Your Goals

Making time for yourself does not need to be over the top, expensive or even to take you out of the house all the time. If you are strategic with your time and brainstorm some ideas, I am pretty sure that you can find simple ways to make yourself a priority again. Make time for yourself so you can maximise your potential.

Constantly giving ourselves and our time to our family drains us a lot. We will eventually become dried up, lacking peace, joy and happiness in our calling. But I know that sometimes, it can be a great challenge to actually make time for ourselves happen.

Some of us are strapped for cash, some of us have partners who work long hours, etc. If you fall into any of those categories, then I hope some of these tips might help you! Because you are important.

2. Look After Your Appearance

1. Wash your face. After I put my children to bed, I always clean my skin and moisturise my face with organic virgin coconut oil. Always wash your face before bed, even if you don't want to. Don't be lazy. Regardless of how tired you are that evening, just do it. I used to buy expensive creams, but now I am using simple jars as cheap as £2.99 and the results are quite amazing.

2. Exfoliate your skin at least once a week, depending on your skin type. To exfoliate, I usually use honey, brown sugar, and squeezed lemon, and then I apply it to my skin. It refreshes my skin and gives a glowing look.

3. I have my own favourite peeling recipe that I prepare myself, which is for cleansing and skin regeneration.

- Take one egg white, and
- One tablespoon of bicarbonate of soda.
- Mix them together.
- Apply to your face and leave it on for five minutes.
- Remove by cleaning your face.

I always stick to my disciplined lifestyle and the importance of making time for myself, setting measurable goals, and keeping a to-do list by my bed. Now, how about if only you could do the same?

3. My Bath Routine

I have my bathing ritual every night. My night routine is to relax at the end of a chaotic day. I take an Epsom salts bath every night to unwind, and I also use a lot of organic essential oils on my pressure points. A pressure-point massage and a bath sounds more like the perfect antidote to a busy day.

4. Screen-Free Zone

I try to keep my bedroom as a screen-free zone. Before bed, my night routine involves leaving my electronics out of the bedroom and opting to read an actual book, before dozing off into a restful sleep. I encourage other women to do the same, as well.

We're going to sleep our way to the top. However, using the last few hours of the day wisely is easier said than done. Who couldn't use a little motivation to set a nightly routine that doesn't involve scrolling through Instagram or re-watching TV shows until an early hour in the morning?

5. Utilise Nap Time

This one was very hard for me to learn and adopt. It's super-easy to catch up on household tasks. You need to rest and fill up your soul, so that you can serve joyfully when those little ones wake up. The dishes can wait, the laundry can sit unfolded, the gardening can be done while children are playing outside.

Allow Your Inner Energy To Be Connected With The Greater Force And

ANYTHING

IS

POSSIBLE.

6. Practise Meditation Or Mindfulness For Guidance

Take time each day to step away from the clutter and the noise. A daily commitment to spend time in a still and quiet place is a commitment to clarity and inner peace. We need this time and space in our lives in order to remember who we really are, what's important, and where our personal truth lies.

It is our time to calm the spirit and soothe the soul. It is also a powerful tool for accessing your creativity, your inner wisdom, and for most people, this means closing your eyes and slowing down your breathing. "Visualise yourself in that peaceful setting.

See and feel your surroundings, hear the peaceful sounds, smell the flowers." Another option: "Imagine being a balloon, floating around the world, watching the earth rotate as you weightlessly move around it."

Does Meditation Work?

Most people have a huge resistance to meditation. They think it's too weird at first, or they're too busy to take the time to learn how to meditate. Focusing on breathing, visualisations, or meditation music can help bring mindfulness to the present moment. This sets the stage to effectively calm your mind.

What Are The Benefits Of Meditating?

Some of the spiritual benefits of meditation include greater awareness of the world around you and a deep connection to yourself and your purpose. Meditate for ten minutes, especially before going to bed or during your daily routine if you can.

This unique type of meditation is defined as a technique for detaching oneself from anxiety and promoting harmony and self-realisation. Just find a comfortable place, close your eyes, relax and recharge your body. Put some relaxing music on in the background and think of every part of your body.

I think of my body when I meditate as being light as a feather. I pay close attention and relax each part of my body. I feel energised afterwards.

7. Love And Relationships

If you want to create an abundance of love in your life, then focus solely on love. Be the love you want to attract. Become more loving and generous with others and with yourself. By creating the vibration of love, you will automatically attract more love into your life.

Direct your focus on whatever it is that you want to create more of in your life, and remember to be grateful for that which you already have. Gratitude itself is a form of abundance.

Once You Find Your IDENTITY, Your PURPOSE, You Have CLARITY.

Chapter 8
Empower Yourself By Improving Your Health

Have A Healthy Regime

First, you have to take care of your health, because health is wealth and remember that the goal is to do this for life, because remaining healthy is something you are required to do as long as you still have breath in you. Healthy body and healthy mind.

REAP THE

REWARD

Of Living A Life To The Fullest.

Daily Morning Routine Habits For An Amazing Start To Your Day

Treat your body like a temple, and not like a trash can. Your body will reward you in a positive way. God gave us our body to take care of, and not to abuse. Good health is the feeling of mental, physical and social well-being, and not only to be free of diseases.

If you are feeling down and at rock bottom, then do yourself a huge favour. You NEED to take proper care of your health. Focus on your health and energy levels at all times. If you take care of your body, it will take care of you in return. Change your diet if needed.

I recommend starting with these simple steps every day:

- Have a wash.
- Brush your teeth.
- Have a good proper breakfast.
- Walk around your neighbourhood with your dog, if you have one.
- Clean your rooms one at a time. Start with a thirty-minute spring clean. When your house is clean and fresh, you are more productive and you feel happier.
- Get enough sleep – aim for eight hours.
- Drink water – at least eight glasses a day.
- Eat fruits and vegetables.
- Eat the right diet and throw out all processed foods.
- Eat the right amounts of protein, healthy fats, and carbohydrates.
- Take supplements every day. Our body doesn't get enough from what we eat daily.
- Think about new thoughts, new emotions, and new behaviours.

These steps seem very simple, but are fundamental. Get up from your bed and make them your daily routine activities. You can add to them gradually. And it will show … your energy levels, motivation, and enthusiasm will change. When you have abundant energy levels and vitality, it's much easier to stay positive, focus on the bigger picture, and achieve your goals and dreams.

Build The Perfect Morning Routine!

Here are my daily morning routine habits for an amazing start to your day. Consistency produces positive results. Learn how to start your day right by using your mornings to boost creativity and productivity. Are you having trouble sticking to or building a morning routine?

It's quite easy to forget about a daily routine when your day is full of tasks and personal obligations. Fortunately, there are simple solutions to this problem.

The trick here is knowing the eight healthy habits to include in your morning routine.

Let's get to it.

Early Morning Preparations

Set yourself up for a less stressful morning by laying out clothes, packing your bag, and making lunches the night before. Doing the work in advance will reduce the pressure of your to-do list.

Let The Natural Light In

Remember when your parents would come into your room and open the blinds and windows for light and fresh air? Natural light does help you to get started on the right foot, aiding in mood and perception, and also enabling the performance of tasks.

This tip is especially helpful if the sun is up, but it's an essential one that you should turn into a regular habit.

Make Up Your Bed

In life, sometimes the smallest of actions can have a powerful impact on your daily success. If you make your bed every morning, you will have accomplished the first task of the day. It will give you a small sense of pride, and it will encourage you to perform another task, and another, and another ... in a twinkle of an eye it will have turned into many tasks completed.

The Importance Of A Healthy Breakfast

One of the best morning habits you can build is to start each day by eating a healthy breakfast that gives you energy and supplies your body with a good amount of nutrients. Here is what my typical breakfast includes. I love breakfast that's enriched with vitamins. It's good for your morale.

Start making it a habit to eat healthy every day. You are what you put inside your body and should never skip breakfast.

- Eat 1 banana first thing in the morning.
- Put 4 to 5 cloves of garlic into organic olive/coconut oil.

Put in a handful of:

- Spinach/rocket salad.
- 1 egg mixed together.
- 1 avocado on the side of the plate.
- 1 glass of fresh orange juice or cappuccino/green tea.
- Take warm organic milk, put in half a teaspoon of turmeric and mix it together.

Schedule Your Day

Without a schedule, it's frighteningly easy to lose sight of what needs doing, and get to the end of the day and realise that you've achieved nothing of importance.

Schedule your day by making out a list of tasks that you want to complete during the day. First, make a list of the tasks you want to accomplish, and that are your main priorities. Second, make a list of the tasks that you want to complete by the end of the day.

Try to be realistic about your tasks instead of just making a long list that would be impossible to complete.

Take Daily Vitamins

Daily vitamins are a must for anyone, and you'll feel much

better about your day if you take them on a consistent basis. Vitamins are essential because they:

- Help build a stronger immune system.

- Ensure your body gets essential nutrients.

- Build stronger bone.

Vitamins can give your body the boost it needs to get started, and help your mind to stay focused throughout the day.

These are supplements I take:

- Omega fish oil 2000mg.

- Probiotic 10 billion (you can get higher than 10billion).

- Vitamin D 3000 iu.

- Evening primrose oil 1000mg.

- Glucosamine sulphate 1500mg for my bones, especially for my ankle.

Have A Glass Of Cold Water With Lemon

Start your day by drinking a glass of lemon water. Make sure that your drinking water is clean and safe by using a quality water filter pitcher.

Start your day by drinking a glass of squeezed lemon water to wake you up faster, which is even better than warm water.

This habit helps you:

- Wake up faster.
- Freshen your breath.
- Get large amounts of vitamins.
- Reduce the feeling of hunger.
- Aid your digestive system.

This is a lot easier to do than it seems, and it's a great way to start your day rolling. All you need to do is pour some water into a glass and add a couple of drops of lemon juice.

Easy, right?

Drink Plenty Filtered Water

Water is hydrating, refreshing, healthy, natural and it contains no calories. It also helps to clear up acne, too! You can also drink freshly squeezed orange juice, because the Vitamin C is really good for your body. Avoid fizzy drinks. They are full of sugar and chemicals, they have tons of calories, and they are fattening.

In other words, soda is just harmful for your body. It's best to drink water, or choose other healthy options such as natural fruit juice.

Expand Your Vocabulary

Learning a new word helps you in the following ways:
- Increases your communication skills.
- Provides a good workout for your brain.
- Boosts your self-confidence in social situations.

Set your homepage to Dictionary.com's "Word of the Day". Subscribe to Wordsmith's A.Word.A.Day and get the featured word daily through your email.

Exercise Daily

A great way to start or end your daily exercise is through a total-body workout. The word "exercise" may make you think of running around big heavy machines at the gym. But it can include a wide range of activities that boost your activity level in order to help you feel much better.

Physical activity, such as gardening, walking around the block or engaging in other less intense activities, can help as well. Anything that gets you off the couch and moving can help to improve your mood throughout your day.

Complete A 15-Minute Workout

Regular workouts can greatly improve your muscle strength and boost your endurance. Exercise delivers oxygen and nutrients to your tissues, regulates blood sugar levels and also helps your cardiovascular system work more efficiently.

Also, when the health status of your heart and lungs improves, you have more energy to tackle daily chores. Your job is to find the right diet that works well for you, and then learn how to maintain it. I like Zumba classes once a week. I alternate with exercise on the vibration machine, which I have at my home.

It's just fifteen minutes, but the benefit is so incredible and you see an instant change in your energy levels. I love it. Not only do you become fit, but you're healthy, too. I also do lots of walking. If I don't have to take the car I choose to go on foot.

How Do You Stay Motivated?

Starting and sticking with an exercise routine can be a challenge. Follow these three simple steps.

1. Identify What You Enjoy Doing

Figure out what type of fitness or physical activities you're most likely to do, and think about when and how you'd be most likely to follow through. For instance, would you be more likely to do some gardening in the evening, start your day with a jog, or go for a bike ride or play football with your friends? Do what you enjoy to help you stick with it.

2. Set Reasonable Goals

Think realistically about what you might be able to do and begin gradually. Tailor your plan to your own needs and abilities, rather than setting unrealistic guidelines that you're unlikely to meet.

3. Don't Think Of Exercise Or Physical Activity As A Chore

Look at your exercise or physical activity schedule the same way you look at your therapy sessions, meditation or massage – as one of the tools to help you get better. Smaller amounts of physical activity – as little as ten to fifteen minutes – make a difference.

Set A Bedtime Routine

Going to bed and waking at the same time each day is the best way to keep your natural body clock in balance. This promotes a regular sleep cycle, which helps to keep the rest of your body processes running smoothly. Sleep for at least eight hours.

Switch off your gadgets and remember turn off your Wi-Fi router, too – you're being exposed to its EMF radiation emissions when you're not even using it! Think about it.

Improve Your Habits

Now, the last piece of advice I want to introduce to your self-care regimen is to improve your habits (both at work and at home). Habits define who- you are, and are built up over time. When you form habits that allow you to progress towards your goals, you're automatically living a purposeful day, every day of your life.

Chapter 9
The Importance Of Keeping A Journal

Keep A Journal And Write For Pleasure

There are lots of incredible ideas just waiting to be materialised with a pen, or a keyboard. All you have to do is just start by putting your thoughts on a piece of paper. This will help you in more ways than one, and it will contribute a lot to understanding yourself better.

Writing Journals

I love the time when I'm left alone with my thoughts. The time of my recovery pen was like my golden pen. I write things down at will. I never thought in a million years that I would use my journals to write a book. NEVER.

If you want to write something, jot it down, otherwise you will forget.

Nowadays, it's so easy as you can use your smartphone. Jot things down whenever you think of them, and nothing gets lost from your creative mind.

Chapter 10
The Power Of Forgiveness

Forgive Yourself And Let Go Of Guilt

Forgive. We've all heard this word before. Forgive yourself and others. When you forgive it's not about the other person; in fact, it's all about you. You're healing yourself. It's easy to say, but so much harder to actually do it! We call ourselves losers.

We all mess up sometimes and those mistakes often come with overwhelming feelings of guilt, shame, self-condemnation, humiliation, and resentment, which only bring bitterness and unhappiness.

It's time to let the negativity go. We have to forgive people's behaviour, and their flaws. None of us on Earth is perfect. It's scientifically proven that negative emotions can lead to stress, depression, anxiety and even heart disease. It's not worth it, is it?

People who forgive are happier people. We live chained to our past, and holding on to hurts and grudges. Learning to forgive is good for your soul and your well-being. Let go of all the grudges. You always win when you forgive.

What To Do When Someone Hates You

Hatred is a hard thing to handle, particularly when you feel it is unjust. "There is only one way to avoid criticism: do nothing, say nothing and be nothing," says Aristotle.

It will also surprise you just how long some people will nurse hatred in their hearts. It can be years later, and they're still hanging onto something that you barely remember. Don't confuse criticism with hate. Criticism comes with putting yourself out there. It happens.

No matter what you do, how kind you are, or anything else, I promise you this: just by being you, you will attract haters. But how do you respond when that criticism turns to hatred? I have created nine helpful tips for you.

Tip 1: Not Every Criticism Is Motivated By Hate

If someone gives you constructive criticism he/she wants to help you improve and become better at what you do. Determine whether the motivation is love or hate by recognising who criticised you and how they gave the criticism to you. What was the intent?

1 insult + 1,000 compliments = 1 insult. This maths doesn't make sense. Reject it. I deal with haters by admitting that there's enough room in this big wide world for both of us to dwell in.

I recall a story of a professor who drew a little "X" in the corner of the whiteboard. Across the board he drew a cloud. He pointed at the cloud and said: "This is the Universe." He walked across the front of the room to the tiny "X" and told the class, "This is you." Then, he said something profound. "Notice that you–" (he pointed at the "X") "–are not at the centre of the universe." (He pointed at the cloud.)

Love is a powerful response to hate.

Tip 2: Centre Your Thoughts In Healthy Ways

I'm not the centre of the universe, none of us is. But we can choose to centre our thoughts daily. When hate rears its ugly head, it hurts us badly. And yet, centring our thoughts gets easier with time. Focus on your goals. We've got things to get done!

Have you ever thought how your life would be different if you stopped allowing other people to dilute or poison your day with their words or opinions? Let today be the day that you stand strong in the truth of your beauty, and journey without attachment to the validation of others.

Tip 3: Focus On Likes, Not On The Haters

You probably can't make the haters like you. Instead, turn your focus on the people who actually do like you. Spend time cultivating those relationships and perhaps they'll come to love you. Focus on helping and serving others and being kind to them.

Choose to ignore those who may be speaking negatively about you – that can quickly become paranoia. Usually, it turns out that people aren't even talking about you at all. Keep perspective and keep to your task. I've read about Theodore Roosevelt saying, "It is not the critic who counts," but why do we give them power over us?

Why should we let haters distract us from living an epic life?

Tip 4: Celebrate Good Times

Every day, we learn and grow. Just a little bit. It's usually imperceptible at the time, which is why it feels like we're not making any progress. But, if you turn back around and look at the person you were ten years ago, you can see how far you've come. A lot has happened in the past decade, and you're going to make a lot happen in the next decade.

If we only ever pay attention to the road ahead of us, we become too focused on the *gap* between where we are and where we want to be. We can become blind to what we've *gained* so far in our journey. All we see is a finish line that's always out of reach. We never feel any closer, like Achilles chasing a tortoise.

When we celebrate our progress as we go, some powerful things happen.

Tip 5: Acknowledge Your Achievements

The celebration when you cross the finish line should be the biggest, but not the only one. If we don't celebrate the work we've already put in, it will quickly start to feel like it's all been for nothing. When you set up the goal, be sure to include the reward at the end – how you're going to celebrate the awesome change you just made to your life!

Tip 6: Make Sure You Like Your Path

In addition to celebrating, pause and reflect. You should be able to see early signs of what the final goal will be like. Don't give up in your life because the going gets tough. Be determined regarding where you want to go. When the going does get tough, it helps you to reconnect with your

"Why".

Feel good. It's our body's natural way to reward progress. By celebrating the gains we have made, we face the time it's taken for us to get this far. Be patient and keep going! We all fail. I fail. You fail. It's part of life.

Tip 7: Accept Correction And Move Forward

Failure becomes permanent only if we stop trying. It becomes success when we learn from it.

But let's be clear about the difference between failure and criticism. Criticism is not failure. Being criticised and having a hater is part of being human. What should you do when someone corrects you?

Stay humble. Do not let pride cause you to reject the correction. On the other hand, do not allow yourself to become overwhelmed with discouragement just because you have something to work on. Humility will help you to avoid either extreme. Remember: the correction that *hurts* the most may be the correction that you *need* the most.

If, for whatever reason, you reject it, you miss out on a valuable opportunity and you don't grow out of that level.

Be thankful. Even if you find the correction difficult to accept, why not express your gratitude to the person who gave it? Undoubtedly, that person has your best interests at heart and truly wants you to succeed.

Tip 8 : Choose Not To Hate

Hating is like tying a dead body to your back – the body doesn't care that it's attached to you, but you bear the burden. Hating hurts the hater most of all. When you are bothered by a person's hatred towards you, it gives them power over you. They can rejoice because they ruined your inner peace and your day.

Their purpose is wounding you and causing you so much pain, and they'd probably be happy even if you were dead. The less you respond to negative people, the more peaceful your life becomes.

Tip 9: Live Life!

Life is too short to make a big deal about a small person. And hate does exactly that – it has a way of making the person on the receiving end feel smaller and less capable of success. Thrive, succeed and enjoy your life to the fullest.

Fulfil your mission and spend time with people you love, especially people who don't have a problem with the fact you're breathing air at this moment.

Forgiveness Isn't About Others, It's About You ...

FORGIVE

AND

MOVE ON.

Chapter 11
The Power Of Prayer

Morning Prayers For Inner Peace

Many times I feel like I am in a battle zone. Time's caught in an endless storm, with thoughts flying out of control. You need the peace deep down in your heart that stays with you day and night and speaks confidently into your soul. I pray to God to help me calm my anxious spirit, all the attacking "if-onlys" and "what-ifs" fill me with unnecessary worry.

You know that trust is a big part of experiencing peace, and that fear has no place in your life. Most of the things you worry about don't even happen. This is how I usually pray:

"Your Presence is Heaven in me, my God. So, I'm declaring my trust in You. I'm releasing the reins of my life and asking You to take control. I need more of You and less of me. I surrender and admit: I can't control people, plans, or even all my circumstances, but I *can* yield those things to You, and focus on Your goodness. Thank You for every good gift You've given, every blessing You've sent, all the forgiveness that I did not deserve, and, yes, by Your grace and mercy, You give them to me. Every trial You've allowed into my life, You bring good out of every circumstance if I'll only let go and believe You. I know that when I pray and give thanks instead of worrying, You have promised that I can experience the kind of peace that passes all understanding. And this is one I crave."

I don't know about you, but I can't start a day without thanking God for the new day He gives, new opportunities, and favour of life. I take ten to twenty minutes to be grateful for everything God has blessed me with. I ask God to protect me, my children, and my loved ones. I plead His forgiveness over my family members, loved ones.

I ask God for wisdom and guidance that everything that I try to do and achieve is according to His plan.

GPS – God's Plan For Significance:
A Roadmap For The Rest Of Your Life

I was thinking about that GPS this morning and the thought came to me that our universe has its own GPS at work in our lives, too. Now, the definition of a GPS is a "Global Positioning System", but I believe that God's system would be called a "God Positioning Spirit".

The Holy Spirit, working in your heart and life, and revealing the Word of God to you on a daily basis is what keeps you on track and headed for your final destination. For a GPS to do you any good, you have to be on the move, going somewhere.

After all, why would I want to know what my position is if all I'm doing is sitting on my backside in a rocking chair? Something has to be programmed into the TomTom or it just sits there and has little use. All of the information that it can give, and all of the directions that are stored there to help you along the journey, don't do one bit of good until a journey is begun.

What concern is it of mine that there is a left turn ahead, if I'm not moving? The point of what I'm trying to say here is that if you are on your way to Heaven, then you must allow the Word of God to guide and direct you on the right way to follow.

Let the Word tell you what road to take, where you need to make adjustment and if the path that you are on is the right one or not. Then you have to let the voice of the Holy Spirit speak to your heart and mind, and then listen to the directions.

You may think that you know better than the TomTom how to get where you want to go. Imagine you just drive into some unfamiliar territory and you'll soon come to realise that you need the help of that tiny little machine. If you've ever had to ask for directions, and been given the wrong directions, you know what I mean.

There's a story I read once of a man and his wife who left for a long trip, no more than a day at most, but it turned out to be much longer before the trip was done. The problem was that this man's wife was always telling him to ask someone for directions.

She was always saying, "Ask that man for directions. He looks like he's from here." Well, her husband grew weary of the constant nagging to ask for directions, so he purposely decided to cure it once and for all. He pretended that he asked and then took the train that he thought was the correct one, but it ended up going in a different direction.

Then they boarded a bus. He went up to the window, and she again gave the same advice: "Ask that man for directions. He looks like he's from here." Then she quickly fell asleep. When she woke up they were in a completely different place. You get the point of this story.

What Us Humans Are Striving For Is A

Deeper Level Of Connection,

One-To-One Communication With Our Creator.

Chapter 12
The Power Of Mindfulness

Update Your Mindset, Reset And Respond

Overcoming obstacles often includes embracing change and learning from past mistakes. To defeat obstacles as they come up, you may need to update your mindset so that you view change as an opportunity and mistakes as lessons to be learned and necessary steps toward success. Examine your "excuses".

Focus on how you can use your knowledge of what doesn't work to deal more effectively with obstacles. We have all heard the saying that it's ten percent of what happens to you and ninety percent how you respond to what happens to you. This is so true! It is perspective that changes the season that you are in and how long you stay in a season.

The move forward can come sooner rather than later for you if you can embrace the proper paradigm shift to overcome the challenge and become empowered by it. So, ask yourself, "How will I let this moment establish me going forward or staying back?"

Block Out Negativity And Focus On The Positive

Diminish your social life so that you can devote yourself to getting out of the hole. Reach out to your network from a place of strength, not desperation.
Build meaningful relationships. Hope plus action takes you to success.

Heal Your Thoughts, Heal Your Life

We are not bound by whips or chains, but by our thoughts, and this is the lifetime to learn how to think! Our thoughts lead us in different directions, to places we want to go and sometimes to places we don't want to go. The key is finding the spiritual action that will assist us in controlling our innermost thoughts.

When we release control of how we think other people should think, feel, or act, we strengthen the connection to our spiritual GPS.

POSITIVE

THINKING

Is A Necessary Attribute To Doing Well.

Stop Being A Chronic Complainer

What do you call a person who complains a lot? Have you ever come across one? I have, and it's very sad. The person is never happy, they are disempowered and unbalanced. They moan and sulk, like spoilt children. They are very hard to please.

You tell them the solution and they come up with impossibility. They present a huge challenge for those around them. And nothing makes chronic complainers happier than being more miserable than their friends or people around them.

A complainer is like a death eater because there's a suction of negative energy.

You can catch a great attitude from great people.

BARBARA CORCORAN

Most chronic complainers truly see their lives as being full of tragedy, hardship and challenge.

Their perceptions about anything are deeply embedded in their personalities and sense of identity. Therefore, although they tell others about their problems all the time, they are not really looking for advice or solutions.

When you advise them how to resolve a problem they will not be especially happy to hear it. They will always come up with "buts" and "ifs", and they will be resistant to a solution, before they even try anything whatsoever. Chronic complainers do not usually see themselves as negative people. Please don't be one of them.

NEVER

Let Anyone Tell You That You Can't.

Surround Yourself with Positive People

The mind is the wall of your heart. People have a huge impact on your life. Some people can be parasites. They suck out your happiness, energy, everything good that is in you, they simply drain you out. Being around negative people will make you more miserable and heavily depressed.

Instead, be around people who really care, people who make you laugh and make you happy, lift your spirit up and are with you in the darkest moments of your life. These are the kinds of people who pull you out of the deepest pit of your life.

They spread positive vibes, enrich your life, and give you confidence. You also have to be yourself. This will lead you to the people that are right for you.

They can be:

- Family members.
- Friends, mentors, specialists.

Positive people inspire you, motivate you to achieve your goals, make the necessary changes you need to succeed and cheer on your success. You'll be less stressed and find more joy in daily things. Try to avoid negative thoughts, because once you embrace them, they will stay with you and become worse.

Choose to reject them and think positive thoughts only. When you're surrounded by good people, you're surrounded by life. Today, make a commitment to start finding and spending time with positive people in your life. Always speak good about yourself, it will help you a great deal. It helped me!

Give Yourself The

FREEDOM

Of Making Mistakes.

Talk About It. You're Not Alone.

When it comes to feeling depressed for whatever reason, silence can be deadly. We are imperfect people, and we make various mistakes in life. We have all hurt people sometimes. We have regrets. It's part of living in a less-than-perfect world.

My advice is, sharing your problems with someone is vital. There are people out there who are happy to help. Stop pretending. Free yourself from the bondage of holding it all in. Talk about what's tearing you apart inside. Express the emotions you feel to a counsellor, mentor, or friend you can trust.

Forgiveness starts with being honest and vulnerable about who you are – good or bad. Say what you need to say. Accept it for what it is and work yourself out.

Find Something You Love
And Are Passionate About,
And Pursue It With
All Your Heart.

How To Be Motivated

If you're going to achieve your deepest dreams and desires, you must understand so well how your mind works. The majority of people are so focused on the negative aspects of their goals that they can't help it.

When you learn how to tap into the deep reserves of your mind, you turn:

- Probability into possibility
- I can't" into "I can" and
- "Can I?" into "How can I?"

The more you focus your mind on what you can do – the easier it becomes. You must realise that your mind is not in control – instead, you are. Keep the big picture in mind. Visualise the results. Be more motivated, more driven, more passionate about your goals.

You have to be positive, and visualise it in your mind. Be positive in everything that you do, even when things don't look good. My life hasn't been a fairy tale. I had my bad times, I had my sleepless nights, I had my cries, my struggles, but I pushed through.

My valuable advice is:

- If you can't run fast, walk.
- If you can't walk, crawl.
- If you can't crawl, push through, keep moving, no matter how slowly, just keep moving ...

We all have our tribulations and adversities. The way you cope is what really matters. I have faced waves of uncertainty in my life, but I didn't let these waves drown me. I found out that it's really not about what comes at you, because we all face various challenges in life, it's really about how we deal with the things that challenge us and how we can allow those challenges to help us to live a more empowered life.

On my journey I learned tribulation, struggles and difficulties make us stronger. We are not on the same level anymore. When you look back and have overcome and prevailed, it makes you think: "Aww, how did I do that?" You rise above the impossible and you become an unbreakable, unshakable and an unsinkable soul!

There are people that go through challenges, but they can't cope mentally, physically, and emotionally.

Know The Definiteness Of Your Purpose

Life has taught me that I must first start with *who I want to be* rather than *what I want to have or accomplish*. I would suggest that many of us don't know ourselves well enough, and early enough, to pursue those things that really serve us well, or use our gifts and talents in the best possible ways.

To be successful in any area of life you must have a "Definiteness of Purpose", meaning that you must have a clear understanding of what you want and it must be a burning desire and a passion. When you have a definiteness of purpose, you will not be distracted by anything that takes you away from pursuing this purpose.

We all know the inspired Nike's greatest ad slogan, "Just do it!" Napoleon Hill says to make up your mind and "start today to go after it. Do it now!" He says: "Successful people move on their own initiative but they know where they are going before they start."

In other words, you have to know the importance of being absolutely definite in connection with your major purpose in life.

If It's Been Done Before, It Can Be Done Again

Every great dream begins with a dreamer. Do you know that saying? One person can change a nation. Yes, I couldn't agree more. One person can do unbelievable things. All it takes is for that one person to risk everything to make it happen.

When I hit rock bottom, my lowest point in life ever, I knew something had to change. But I didn't know what I needed to change. So, I spent weeks listening to stories of successful people who had seemingly lost everything and still achieved success, and many other success icons who were once in a deeper pit.

I started to go to different events, one after the other, to listen to successful people. I bought their programmes. I was determined that I wasn't going to stop until I landed somewhere. I didn't want any more procrastination. And every single day, I looked at myself in the mirror and reminded myself that, "If it's been done before, it can be done again."

If someone has overcome the situation that you are in, so can you. You have the power to achieve success beyond your wildest dreams. You have the power to get out of rock bottom and climb to the apex of the mountain. But you need to remind yourself of this truth daily.

Remember: one book, one pen, one child, and one teacher can change the world. When the world is silent, even one voice becomes powerful. You, too, are enough to change the world!

Summary

Born To Stand Out, Not To Fit In is for anyone who wants more out of life. Learn how to live the life-changing strategies, unlocking and unleashing the forces inside of you to break through limitations and finally create the life you want beyond success, one full of purpose, joy, and personal fulfilment. It is for you if you are looking to find your true life purpose.

My true desire in writing this book is to inspire others by converting my deep-rooted, tested, fact-based experience and beliefs into a compelling message that will empower and enable people to make a difference to their lives, and the lives of others, also.

I have learnt and developed over the years and I hope you will benefit from this book. I know it may not attract everyone, and that's okay, since my interest is to attract people who share the same core beliefs and values as me. The reward is enormous and priceless! That's when my personality serves my soul, my Authentic Power!

About The Author

Teuta Avdyli is an empowerment, spiritual and positive parenting coach. Teuta overcame difficult situations, such as coming to London as a refugee, fleeing difficult conditions, getting almost drowned in the sea on the way, struggling to conceive children, getting run over by a lorry in London.

She overcame all that against all odds through a positive consistent attitude, by becoming spiritually awakened and by looking after herself with the techniques she shares in this book. She is the mother of two children, and is on the way to becoming an international speaker, inspiring thousands of people with her stories of overcoming adversity.

In *Orphan's Promise Project*, she has offered monthly financial help for the well-being of orphans and vulnerable children around the world by providing food, shelter, medical help, academic opportunity, and health programmes.

In *Successful Mothers Platform*, she helps to empower mothers in order to overcome adversities and struggles. She meets up with other successful mothers every month and shares their vision to help others.

I have prepared a special masterclass blueprint for you as I would like to help you stay on track in your empowerment journey and also so that you can start practicing these tools I spoke about in the book.

Watch the FREE masterclass here:
www.teutaavdyli.com/masterclass

I would be most grateful if you could leave a review on Amazon for me.
Hope to meet you someday!
You can subscribe to my social media channels:

Instagram: @teutaavdyli
LinkedIn: Teuta Avdyli
Facebook: Teuta Avdyli
YouTube: Teuta Avdyli
Podcast: The Empowerment Podcast

42304790R00132

Printed in Poland
by Amazon Fulfillment
Poland Sp. z o.o., Wrocław